SUCCEED WILDLY IN COLLEGE!™

Achieve More in College & Career Than You Ever Thought Possible!

Discover the *Do 27 Not 25* Method to Success

David A. Leis

SUCCEED WILDLY IN COLLEGE!™

*Achieve More in College & Career
Than You Ever Thought Possible!*

DAVID LEIS

SUCCEED WILDLY IN COLLEGE!™

Achieve More in College & Career Than You Ever Thought Possible!

Discover the *"Do 27 Not 25"*™ Method to Success

Avantt Press

**Published by Avantt Press
Princeton, New Jersey, USA**
www.succeedwildlyincollege.com

ISBN: 1941172008
ISBN-13: 9781941172001
Library of Congress Number: 2014900134
Avantt Press, Pennington, NJ

Cover Design: Judy Bullard www.customebookcovers.com
Author Photo: Dan Naylor www.dannaylor.com

Copyright © 2015 by David A. Leis
All Rights Reserved No part of this publication may be reproduced, stored in a retrieval system or transmitted by any means, electronic, mechanical photocopying, recording or otherwise without the prior permission in writing of the publisher, except by a reviewer who may quote brief passages in a review.

Printed in the United States of America

To the faculty and students of the colleges where I have taught. I learned so much more from you than I taught you. I am honored to have been entrusted to be in your classrooms. Thank you. I wish you the very best.

And to Don and Norma Leis, my parents, part of the Greatest Generation, from whom I learned the most important lessons of my life reflected in these pages.

ACKNOWLEDGMENTS

I owe a tremendous debt of gratitude to so many people I hardly know where to begin. This book was written on my many three-hour commutes into New York City, including one-hour train rides where I could put pencil to paper. I want to thank Mr. Mario Federici and the great faculty of FIT (Fashion Institute of Technology) in New York for the opportunity to teach there and finally put into writing the mini lectures I had been giving in other college classrooms and corporate settings for twenty years.

That journey began with mentoring from David Quattrone, Chairman of the Business Division, who hired me and later Jayne Peaslee, and the wonderful faculty and staff at Corning Community College to whom I am indebted. Both of those colleges are absolute jewels in higher education that I am proud to have been part of along with some other really fine colleges I had the opportunity to occasionally teach for at some point including Cazenovia College, Empire State College, Canisius College and Keuka College.

But the gratitude goes beyond that, as there have been so many people supporting me on the journey. That begins with John and Joan Bickel who have supported me for many years in ways beyond what anyone could expect from friends.

Unbounded love goes to my daughter, Sharon who read my manuscript and encouraged me, as well as my two sons, John David, who worked alongside me every step of the way, and Stephen, who simply loved me every day.

I want to thank Ed Gaffney, my dear friend, who read the manuscript and provided great feedback, and Marcel Floss, a stellar student at FIT who provided awesome feedback and proved that a rail-thin guy could in fact eat a two-pound rib eye steak! (guys check out www.onedapperstreet.com for your wardrobe!) Oh, yes, and thanks to my other students whose names you will see in the book, on the website, and marketing materials.

People like Steve Harrison, Geoffrey Berwind and Martha Bullen from Bradley Communications and Jack Canfield, co-author *of Chicken Soup for the Soul*, provided a great deal of professional guidance without which I would never have had the confidence to publish. The title and subtitle I credit to that team. Mary Lou Warren was there during the critical phase of actually turning my notes into a book and helping me get it turned into a project. I also had the good fortune to run into Bill Bartmann along the way who inspired me with his tenacity at overcoming obstacles. Appendix D is devoted to that lesson.

There are a whole host of clients from my consulting who were the early recipients of the mini lectures that accompanied each of these handouts during some form of consulting engagement, including strategic planning or training. They include Corning, Inc., Welliver-McGuire, Toshiba, Ancoma, Davenport & Taylor Hospital, Dietrich's, Hunt Engineers, Sepac, Southern Tier Custom Fabricators, Steuben ARC, and ETG, Inc. to name a few.

Last, not least, and foremost, I thank God, my Creator who has been so generous and gracious to me. I am humbled by it, for I certainly do not deserve it. But that is gratuitous gift, isn't it? He has blessed me with family, friends, coworkers, and mentors who have all supported me. God has given me everything that I have and am, including the courage and stamina to pursue this dream against all odds. To Him be praise forever!

With loving gratitude,
David A. Leis

So you want to be a success, wildly successful?
That is why you are in college?
Here is a secret:
Success, wild success, can be yours
…if you separate yourself
from the average that surrounds you
and breeds a culture of mediocrity.
It took a long time to become who you are today.
What got you to where you are today
is not going to get you where you need to go
to be successful in the future.
You have boundless untapped potential within you
just waiting to be unleashed!
But you cannot be who you were yesterday.
Nor can you be who you are today
if you are to live to your potential.
That is inadequate for your future success.
Otherwise, you would not be in college, right?
Make a few meaningful decisions now.
Change your habits of thought.
Start becoming who you intend to become.
A few small decisions now
will have a *huge* impact later.
It will take a long time
to become who you need to be.
So be it—starting now!

WHAT OTHERS HAVE TO SAY:

OK, you are about to find out that this book is unconventional. It is not like any other book you have ever read, as what I do in class is not what any other professor does, according to my students.

So rather than some short quotes by a lot of other people, I just have a few stories from some of my students. I think they speak for themselves and hopefully will assist you in understanding why the book is SO very important to your future!

It's professors like David Leis who can take a class you debate about going to (even if you do have a lot of catching up to do on the Internet), to a class you look forward to going to. Every class began with a quote, something inspirational or thought provoking, that talked of success, teamwork, happiness, and various aspects of life. The class wasn't about the textbook; it was about something more tangible: thoughts, ideas, and growth. He would ignite the dialogue but we were directing the discussion. It was on us to come to our own conclusions about the topic. It's one thing to have a professor stand in front of the class and tell you want he or she wants you to think, but it's another when you find it on your own. With these discussions you find meaning for yourself on how to live your life the way you need to. You define your life; you define your success.

Leaving each class I felt different, as if I had one more block to help me shape my future, my goals. You can't let other people pave your road to success. You have to lay it out yourself, brick by brick.

—*Taylor Ruckh, Senior*

WHAT OTHERS HAVE TO SAY:

The most important lessons that Professor Leis taught me were not how to create an impeccable pivot table in Excel, although he also did that, but he taught me that my choices matter. He didn't teach me this in a way that a lecturing parent tells their child the first day they get their driver's permit, but every class he reiterated that my choices matter because I matter, and my generation matters.

Below I will try to explain the significance of the semester spent in Professor Leis' class.

I showed up to Professor Leis' class dreading the Information Technology class that was required for graduation. As a college student in New York City, I was already feeling the pressures of the ambitious city. I showed up to class with my yoga mat from the 6:00 a.m. morning class I had taken, wearing heels from the internship I came from, and carrying another bag for work clothes because I was headed straight to my part-time restaurant job after class. Now that I've described a picture of how overloaded I was physically, imagine all of those bags on a petite frame, times ten, and that's how emotionally overloaded I felt on that snowy afternoon.

As I headed into the classroom I was in the midst of holding back tears. I plopped myself down in the second row and watched as professor Leis greeted every student with a quirky smile. Professor Leis took an extra look at me as I sat there and rather than asking if I were OK, he handed me a paper with an anonymous quote. Once the remaining students took their seats, he asked me to read the quote in front of the entire class. I thought to myself, "This guy is such a jerk," but bitterly obliged to do so. He stopped me multiple times and asked me to reread several of the lines. I had to bite my innately quick tongue before brashly replying, "Did I stutter or are you deaf?" Slowly I began to understand that neither were the answer to my pointed question, but he was waiting for me to actually read the quote. My urge to cry my eyes out and give up on my dreams after another terrible day at my seemingly terrible internship slowly dissipated and I started to reread the lines to the class without being asked to do so.

As the weeks continued, myself and other students started arriving to class five minutes early and by the end of the semester most of the students were in their seats at least thirty minutes prior to lecture taking place. During these thirty minutes, Professor Leis would listen to us banter back and forth and vent about our jobs, internships, and excessive homework. Most of the time he would remain silent and look up a few times to smile at us from behind his computer, but would just let us say whatever we felt was necessary. One day a classmate asked, "Professor Leis, doesn't that suck?" In that instance, Professor Leis didn't smile, but he got up from behind his desk

WHAT OTHERS HAVE TO SAY:

and pulled a chair up next to our chatting circle, and said, "No." We all exchanged glances that, if translated into words, would have the significance of, "I thought this guy was supposed to be cool." He sat calmly and explained how our choices mattered. Our choices during the thirty minutes prior to class to sit and complain mattered and our choices to do things that we weren't passionate about mattered, and more importantly, our attitude about everything mattered. We had gotten Professor Leis' first lecture on positive thinking. For the remainder of that class period we sat in unusual silence as we pondered what we had been told. For the remainder of the semester we continued to show up to class early, but rather than discussing how much our bosses sucked or how annoying professor so and so was, we talked about future job possibilities, how we didn't like a lot things that had gone on at our internship, but we loved one thing. Slowly, our positive thinking became contagious.

Although, it's a lifelong lesson, my classmates and I have slowly started to take this positive thinking outside of the classroom and apply it to our daily lives. Professor Leis has the uncanny ability to relate to college students on a personal level in professional manner.

—Rose Gamelsky, Junior

Professor Leis' lectures truly opened my eyes to the world outside the classroom. I was inspired to do my best in class and in my daily activities in life. His mini lectures were a great way to start my day and motivate me to shoot for the stars. I would hang them on refrigerator each week and my roommates would be inspired as well. I am so happy to have taken his class.
—Kaitlyn Kuchler, Freshman

I took Professor Leis' class in my first semester at Fashion Institute of Technology.

I came to the United States from St. Petersburg, Russia, and was always looking forward to an education at a school like FIT. But considering cultural and language differences, I wasn't always sure that I could be a successful student.

When I finally started my classes, I tried my best to adapt to the American system of education, which is completely different from what I was used to in Russia. Professor Leis happened to be one of my teachers, and I consider myself very lucky! His classes were very interesting and I looked forward to them, especially because of the little inspiring talks he gave us each week! It was his intention to give us positive energy and meaningful guidance that we could use in life. He explained how important it is to be attentive to our thoughts and attitudes.

WHAT OTHERS HAVE TO SAY:

I was slightly older than other students in my class, and after having some experience in adapting by myself in a foreign country, I saw how important his message was. Looking outside of your comfort zone to find your way, without fear and doubts, is the best and only way that we all can use to transform dreams and goals into reality.

Professor Leis was talking straight to our inner "I am" and tried to awaken and encourage us to change what we surround ourselves with. I felt extremely inspired by Professor Leis' talks and the way he tried to show us reality. I believed in myself even more and ended that semester with really great grades, which I was very proud of. Those grades and the level of confidence I gained from those talks helped me to realize that I can take more classes and add an internship.

We create our thoughts and attitudes, projecting them right into our lives, and the results are amazing. I'm very happy that there are people like Professor Leis, who try to remind us about it and help us to stand against the crowd and the culture of mediocrity.
—Natalia Belik, Sophmore

I've learned so much from you and I know I will take all the lessons with me for the rest of my life. It was always just what I needed to get me through the week. I'm so

thankful for everything you did and taught me. You really inspired me to stop being reactive and just really think about what I say and do. You're the best!
—*Apryl C., Freshman*

You made a huge impact on me and my experience in college. I have changed my approach to study and participation in campus activities. My grades are higher than I ever thought I could achieve. And two of the chapters in this book bring me to tears when I read them, they are so powerful.
—*Marcel Floruss, Junior*

The things Professor Leis taught me have had a huge impact on my life! Doing my best no matter who noticed or how I felt about my job. Doing the best job I can possibly do is good for me and that is enough! I was just a stocking clerk in a drug store, while I was in college. But I made such an impression on both the manager and one of the district managers from a supplier, that one day, the DM asked me if I would be interested in joining his company. Great salary, benefits, company car and cell! That only happened because of the lessons Professor Leis taught me.
—*John C., Sophomore*

WHAT OTHERS HAVE TO SAY:

God in His providence introduced me to Professor Leis at a really difficult time in my life. I was unemployed, discouraged, and in need of godly counsel. The first time I heard Professor Leis speak about life, I immediately noticed that his advice was based on the truth of the Bible (that was my interpretation since he never once mentioned God or anything religious), and as a result, it was very applicable to my circumstances.

His encouragement for us to be the best people that we could be for those around us was a blessing. Personally, he helped me to understand that by focusing on being that person, the person that God designed me to be, I could be and will be a hero (a refreshing and helpful presence) to those around me. Additionally, his advice was practical and well received by everyone in the class because of his relationship with the Lord and his love for people.

Professor Leis also showed me that part of being the best person we can be is recognizing what we do bring to the table and not undervaluing our own abilities. This advice proved invaluable because it helped me to successfully negotiate a contract with a major global luxury brand for much-needed work that came my way just a few short weeks after our class ended. I highly encourage you to read this book and to share it with your friends and family. From what I know about the author, I believe this book will inspire and motivate

SUCCEED WILDLY IN COLLEGE!

many people who are in the valley or going through setbacks. It will lead them to examine their lives and will help them on their journey to become who they were meant to be.

—C. Webber,
Graduate Career Certificate Program

TABLE OF CONTENTS

Acknowledgments ·ix
What Others Have to Say: · xv
Preface · xxvii
Foreword by Robert R. Neuman, PhD · · · · · · · · · · · · · · · · xxix

Introduction to Habits of Thought · 1
Week 1: Your Habits of Thought Determine
         Your Destiny · 13
Week 2: What's Even More Important Than
         Your Education? · 27
Week 3: Wait! The Purpose of Life is Not Happiness? · · · · · · · 37
Week 4: New Ways to Really Believe in You! · · · · · · · · · · · · · · 47
Week 5: Your Real Job Description: Not What You
         Think It Is · 57
Week 6: The Bottom Line: No One Owes You
         Anything! Go for it! · 69
Week 7: You Know a Tree by Its Fruits · · · · · · · · · · · · · · · · · · 79
Week 8: Dare Mighty Things—Or Snivel and Whine! · · · · · · · · 89
Week 9: One of the Most Powerful Tools You Possess · · · · · · · 99
Week 10: A Winner's Blueprint for the Achievement
          of Success · 111
Week 11: Don't Quit · 121

Week 12: Children (And Employees) Learn What
     They Live ·································· 129
Week 13: Consult Not Your Fears ························ 141
Week 14: That Spark of Inspiration Within You? ············ 151
Take *Do 27 Not 25!* to the Next Level ···················· 159
Appendix A: The Dreams for Your Life ··················· 161
Appendix B: SMART Goals and Goal-Setting ············· 163
Appendix C: Action Plans ····························· 169
Appendix D: Dealing with Failure ······················· 173
About the Author ··································· 177

A note to the reader: in the book, I use the word *professor* as college students called me *Professor Leis*. To be clear, I was both an adjunct professor and an associate professor where I taught, but did not stay long enough to attain the rank of full professor. The term is used with that distinction.

PREFACE

In teaching thousands of students in a half dozen colleges and corporate leaders for more than thirty years, I have met an amazing array of people, from the pinnacles of corporate and government leadership to students just starting their journey of learning requisite career skills and knowledge. I have also been privileged to meet and been fascinated by the stories and lives of everyday people, engineers, clerks, dentists, farmers, lawyers, workers in factories, migrant workers and the homeless on the streets. To a person, what they have in common is the desire to live to a greater level of potential than where they were at that moment.

The lessons in the book you are about to read have come from a number of sources. First, I have learned some of the lessons they contain the hard way, from failure first, and then only after that, by mending my ways and doing it right.

Second, my mom and dad, part of the Greatest Generation that fought in and supported those who fought in World War II, were heroes of immense proportions who taught me by their simplicity and humility. I hope someday to achieve a very small part of who they were. Their lessons of hard work, honesty, community, generosity, faith, love, and family stand as unassailable monuments in the turbulence of our society. They are lessons every generation can live by.

Third, these lessons were originally presented in corporate training programs on leadership, management, and team work in my over twenty years of experience as a consultant in some of the largest corporations in the world as well as many small businesses.

Fourth, they were used in the classroom in various colleges, in one form or another, with thousands of students. It was in both the corporate environment and the classroom environment that I received some amazing feedback on these lessons.

These lessons have been credited with changed lives, careers, family life, on and on. Why? Because people took the time to think about them and apply them to their lives. It is to their credit and not mine that such magnificent changes occurred. "When the student is ready, the teacher will appear," I believe is the adage.

I share these lessons with you, the college student, in the hope that you can fail less at these lessons than I have and that you can succeed far more than you ever thought possible. Succeed wildly on your own terms, for who you are and your own potential, as I have seen some of my former students do.

FOREWORD BY ROBERT R. NEUMAN, PHD

During my twenty-five years as a dean in higher education, both advising and teaching students, I have learned a lot about what it takes to succeed. Success in college requires more than great high school grades and high standardized test scores.

The successful college students I've seen over the years have several things in common, one of which is a complete sense of self.

What does that mean? Do you have it, or not? If not, how do you get it?

The book you hold in your hands guides you in answering these questions. *Succeed Wildly in College* defines the *self* and explains how you can develop a self that will succeed in college as well as in life after you graduate.

A college professor himself, author David Leis draws on years of experience teaching and mentoring college students. Like me, he has discovered that to get the most out of a college education, students must be particularly aware of themselves every day. It's a habit to be cultivated—students need to focus seriously and carefully on such self-evaluating questions as these:

- What kind of person am I?

- Do I know how to set personal goals that will produce the future I want?

- When I identify my goals, what do I do to accomplish them?

- Do I seriously try to become a better person each day?

- What does it mean to succeed?

David Leis helps you tackle these questions in a very methodical and practical way. As he says, "Self-discovery does not just happen." Like all important things in your life, you have to work at it. In *Succeed Wildly in College,* you'll learn how to start out on the right foot in your journey of self-discovery.

As you begin to learn about yourself, you'll want to learn more each day. In the end, you'll be able to say, "This is who I am. I know my place in life. I know how to set goals and meet them, and I'm confident I will achieve them with *wild* success."

In short, the better you know yourself, the better student you'll be. David Leis' book will show you how to discover your potential, expand your intelligence about life, and enter your future with confidence and a great deal of self-satisfaction.

~ Dr. Bob
Robert R. Neuman, PhD

Robert R. Neuman
Academic Dean (retired)
Marquette University
Author of *Are You Really Ready For College? A College Dean's 12 Secrets of Success—What High School Students Don't Know*

INTRODUCTION TO HABITS OF THOUGHT

This book was written for all college students and high school seniors who sense that you have more capability, higher aspirations, and a longing to do more than others know, perhaps even your closest friends and family.

It is an unapologetic attack on mediocrity and accepting average results for yourself, settling for less than achieving your full potential as a human being, all that you are capable of being. You will be challenged to look hard at your dreams and aspirations and confront boldly the barriers within you that cause you to accept less than you have the power to achieve. With dispassionate objectivity you will be pushed to assess the parts of the culture and environment around you that distract you from maintaining a vision of the highest goals you have and working every day to achieve them.

There is no room here for living little, for blaming, escaping or excuses. Your highest potential as a human being calls out to you to lay aside the past, the mediocrity of the current culture and to pick up the tools and ways of winning achievement. You were born to be free, happy and fulfilled in your pursuits in this life, not accepting anything that sabotages that. But so many do not achieve that; just look around you. Why? Because for many, average and unfulfilled is all they have known.

For you, it will not be so, if you pursue your full potential with a passion, living an inspired life each and every day, no matter what is going on around you.

That is the purpose of this book, to act as a guide and accelerate your progress along the path you choose to the fulfillment of your potential. But that pursuit is a paradox: you pursue your full potential as gift to those in your life to achieve your greatest fulfillment as a human being. The force by which you are driven is the love of others that is greater than your self-love. For that you exercise your God-given talents and skills, to leave your legacy for the human race! What greater thrill and sense of accomplishment is there? Live an inspired life! The world desperately needs your full potential to lift it up higher.

Remember the definition of insanity? Doing the same thing you have always done and expecting different results. For the purpose of this book, we are about changing the way you think so that you get different results. The methods used here have been proven over decades and confirmed by the latest findings of the science of neuroplasticity. We are about to rewire your brain for greater achievement than you have been taught to expect of yourself using the principles of neuroplasticity. The recent discoveries of this science have revealed that we can deliberately rewire our brains to think our way to a better life. Read Dr. John Arden's "Rewire Your Brain" for some astonishing insights.

There is a method to the process in the book, backed by the science of neuroplasticity, which begins with introducing some foundational new concepts such as habits of thought and why it is so important. A couple of chapters have some self-assessments built in to help you determine where you need to make some changes. Every chapter has a HOT Point – a habit of thought that you can remember easily to help rewire your brain for greater achievement. The last few chapters are oriented to help you then find the inspiration and spark that will become flame to carry you through the inevitable difficulties and failures to achieving your goals.

Lastly, the Appendices are just as important as the rest of the book, maybe more so, because they lay out pragmatic tools that you can use in college to achieve more than you thought possible. And here's the secret: if you use those goal achievement tools in college and get really good at using them, they will become very powerful tools to help you achieve more in your career than you ever thought possible. I have taught thousands of people in my career and have met very few who were at first masters of the material you will find in the Appendices. Those who applied themselves to those materials, however, have found success that surprised even themselves.

One of the secret formulas of success, however you measure it for yourself, is to lay the foundation and develop the structure that eliminates the self-defeating behaviors and replaces them with habits, thinking and structures that support your goals. If you work through this book cover to cover, you will have an uncommon set of tools, and a fresh, new way of thinking, and habits that will give you a better foundation for achieving more than you may have ever thought possible.

Somewhere inside, perhaps deep within yourself, you harbor dreams of a better life, filled with happiness and fulfillment, a desire to be successful—on your own terms.

What will happen to those dreams and aspirations to be better than _____ (you fill in the blank) if you want to be a success? Will you harbor them, nursing them but in time letting them die of cynical neglect? That is what happens to the vast majority of your classmates. Then later in life, regret and resentment rise from the ashes of the dreams, to condemn and belittle the one who once had hope but did not act.

Maybe you will nurse them and work on those dreams, but the realities and experiences of life will so derail you that you eventually give up on them. You might find yourself either living someone else's dreams or just living the life you have and making the best of it with good times, however you define that.

Or will you make those higher aspirations, those secret dreams you harbor within for success and fulfillment a reality? That's the catch. *How* does one go about doing that, other than by brute force or hard work (a necessary element, but not the key)? A few of your classmates will do the things that are necessary to achieve some degree of those aspirations and dreams. You hold a composite of keys that have been tried and tested in achieving uncommon success in achieving the full potential of who you are. You can join those who have realized their aspirations.

By the way, I am not talking about success in terms of money or fame or position or any of that as the 'world' defines it. That may come, but the success I am talking about is the success that only you can measure because it is the fulfillment of your human potential. Trying to define your success by someone else's standards is futile and will only lead to that resentment and regret I talked about earlier.

So here you are in college. No one comes to college intent on becoming a failure. Most do not come to college intent on being mediocre. Most come to college desiring success.

You are at a turning point in your life. You alone have the power to determine the script and the outcome. No one else can do it for you. And you have the power within you to dare to hope enough to make those dreams a reality.

But you have to make some decisions about the way you think, your habits of thought. Now.

Read on to understand the urgency! And those decisions are countercultural, counter the culture of mediocrity. They go against the popular trends. And they go against your very nature, your humanity, in some instances.

Think about a rocket or an airplane flying halfway around the world. Just a small change at the start of the flight will result in a very large change in the end—it can make even a whole continent's difference. Think about a bullet fired toward a target. A small decision about direction and how the trigger is pulled makes the difference in whether the target is hit or missed. So it is with your decisions about your life.

But those decisions need to be made right now. It is more urgent than you can believe.

Why?

Because it took you a long time to become who you are right now. It will take a long time for you to become who you need to be. And you do not have any time to waste getting started.

And who you need to be is not who you are now—that is inadequate for your future success, remember? Which is why you are in college, right?

If you make a few very meaningful decisions about the ways you think, your attitudes, and outlook and start becoming who you need to be, then you will be that better self you need to be when you need to be that.

INTRODUCTION TO HABITS OF THOUGHT

All those aspirations you have for your life and your future? Let's put some muscle into making those things happen in a brand new way, a new approach to achieving what you want for your life. Let's go further in unlocking the potential within you than you ever thought possible.

Is that possible? Even for you?

Yes!

I have seen it and witnessed its effects on thousands of my students from all over the world. It is not a dream. It is tried and proven, for anyone, no matter what your previous experience and life circumstances, no matter how successful or unsuccessful you have been. It has worked miracles in my own life. It can in yours. In fact, it *has* to work because from here forward, the way you think (your habits of thought) will be completely changed if you do everything outlined.

Forever.

That change needs to start now as a college student. Then you will be who and what you need to be when you graduate and start a job. And become a parent. And become a community leader and…

Get it?

Success does not start someday. It starts *now*, right where you are.

"When the student is ready, the teacher will appear," as they say. Are you ready?

Are you ready to make a few simple decisions that will have a very big impact? Are you ready to make the commitment necessary to succeed?

Then let's go!

———

This book is the first in a series and is intended to be read first, most likely in the fall semester of college. Of course, it can be started any time. You can read it and do it during the summer, for instance. It would be exceptionally beneficial for high school seniors who want to make the most of their college experience.

Before you start, one quick note. Jump to the section entitled "Take Do 27 Not 25! to the Next Level." You will want to start on those activities during Week 1 and continue working on them as you go through the book. And read Appendix D as well.

The book has fourteen chapters or "weeks" in this case. If you are in college, there is one for each week of the first semester of the academic year. Almost. Read Week 1 before the first week of class. Then read one a week for the entire semester. Skip finals week. You get the picture.

Otherwise, if you find yourself in a different situation, I would recommend reading and doing just one chapter a week. Don't rush it. Read on to understand why.

If you really want to have an impact on your life, read the same "week" chapter every day of the week. Let it really sink in. You will be amazed at the results.

INTRODUCTION TO HABITS OF THOUGHT

"Really, professor?"

Yeah. There's a huge body of research around something called *spaced repetition*. If you do the same thing, like read something, every day for seven days, it becomes planted deep in your brain. Your retention goes way up from just one reading. So try reading the chapter every day for a week. It will become part of you. After all, it is how you learned math and reading, right?

And if you really want the maximum impact, add tactile (touch) learning to your visual learning. Type the quote or saying up, print it, and put it on your wall. Look at it a few times a day.

At the end of every week's chapter you should reach a point where habits need to be firmly reinforced in your brain to make the slight change that will produce the successes you want for your future. After years of teaching that point where habits are altered forever has become known as a *"HOT Point"* - a *Habits of Thought Point*. It is a term you should repeat to yourself and use throughout this study course. It is a term you should use throughout life because there will be times in your career where you need to once again break away from the mediocre and alter your habits of thinking about some challenge you face. You will then be able to create your own *HOT Points* to lift your thinking to the next level. See how it works? You are the catalyst for change because you establish a *HOT Point* and act on it.

Brilliant huh? Ok, but cool, right? You become the catalyst of the decisions about your thinking that will affect your college success, your future, and your career.

I cannot stress enough how important it is for you to take time to consider the questions at the end of each week carefully, reflect on them, and answer them as best you can. Write down what your first impulse is, and don't spend time editing it. The questions are critical to changing your habits of thought into what you want them to be for success as you define it. Do not make the mistake of glossing over them. That will immediately sabatoge your efforts to change your habits of thought (HOT).

Then lastly there is a *HOT Resolution* to help you make a commitment to your success. Think about it carefully, make the resolution, and then write it down. Do whatever you have to do to remind yourself of that resolution every day.

So simple.

So little effort.

But *so* powerful!

DO 27 NOT 25 HABITS OF THOUGHT (HOT) POINT™: WARM-UP

The following questions are meant as a warm-up to the scheduled weekly exercises. A separate *Succeed Wildly in College Planner* and workbook is available for you to use if you prefer not to write them in the book. This companion planner and notebook reinforces the success principles, provides space for notes, and keeps your dreams, goals, HOT Point answers, and HOT Resolutions private. See the website for more information: www.succeedwildlyincollege.com.

1. Can you list twenty of the dreams you have for your life?

2. List ten dreams you have for your time at college.

3. What do you want most from your college education? What benefits? List ten.

Do 27 Not 25 Habits of Thought (HOT) Point Resolution. Here is a list, a picture of what I want my life to be, a vision for the rest of my life:

WEEK 1:

YOUR HABITS OF THOUGHT DETERMINE YOUR DESTINY

Watch your thoughts;
they become words.
Watch your words;
they become actions.
Watch your actions;
they become habits.
Watch your habits;
they become character.
Watch your character;
it becomes your destiny.

—Lao Tzu

"Destiny? Destiny? Hey, man, I am just a college student, enjoying my life away from home for the first time and you are talking to me about destiny? Come on, professor!"

Yeah, that's right. Destiny. Isn't that why you came to college in the first place, because you are concerned about your destiny enough to get an education? Or are you in college just to get away and party (which is probably true for most people)?

OK, I get it. The last two reasons for going to college are not the overriding reasons (well, maybe they are, just for now). But what about in the big picture?

So work with me. You are getting an education because you have some degree of concern about your destiny. And therefore, you need to train your brain to think in educated ways. That's great. Go for it. Get as much education as you can. Work as hard as you can and get the best grades you can. That is important, believe me.

But it is not enough to get you the destiny you are harboring in your dreams. And it is not enough to fulfill your potential.

Destiny is a result of what we do and how we think. The interesting thing is, what we do is a result of how we think. Got it?

"Hmm. Let me think about that one, professor."

Good idea.

Consider the implications of that. That could take you ten years or so. Even the rest of your life!

Did you come to college to be a failure in life? How about to be mediocre or average in life? Or did you come to college to be a success, to fulfill your dreams, and to discover your potential?

By the way, here is the shocker: your *habits of thought* become your destiny, whether those habits of thought are intentionally formed or whether you just let them happen to you. Think about what I just said very carefully. Intentionally or unintentionally, your habits of thought become who and what you will be. Read that again *slowly*.

Think about that one. Actually, it could not be otherwise, right?

You have unintentional habits of thought. Are they good and uplifting for you or counter-productive to your life's goals?

You can have intentional habits of thought that will program you to move in the direction of your life's goals. You get to choose! Most people do not.

You are about to begin a new life habit: choose your habits of thought with intentional purpose. Wow!

MY DESTINY IS HOT!

Burn this into your brain, "My destiny is the sum of all my habits of thought."

Underline that. Highlight it.

Want to change your destiny? You can choose *Intentional Habits of Thought* to create your destiny! In other words, "I-HOT = Destiny" Cool or what?

Now, observe yourself as you think. Are those thoughts you are having aligned with the destiny you want for yourself? Or are they counter-productive? Replace the negative with the positive.

It is not only the information you absorb while you are at college that shapes your destiny. It is also the way you think, because it drives your words and actions, which become habits.

Stop.

Habits. We all have them, for better or for worse.

Some work for us, others do not. Some habits are not beneficial to our success. Do you know which ones are beneficial and which ones are not?

What is in the head and the heart is manifested in the words we use and in our actions. What is there are our habitual ways of thinking and our attitudes. It is your ways of thinking that result in the outcomes for your life. You deserve the best outcomes, but only you can do what is necessary to get those.

Let me tell you a story about promotions at work when I was working in some big companies. Many times people came to me wanting a chance to move to the next higher level. They wanted me to give them a chance. Sometimes I could not. I could not give them a chance. Why? Because they weren't *it*. They were not what they needed to be.

The reality of promotions is that they are merely the recognition of what you already are.

If I promoted someone who wasn't *it* already, then they would have no credibility with their superiors, their peers, or the people they supervised. Likewise, I would have no credibility with my peers, subordinates, or my superiors.

Of course, you have to show promise that you will develop to be even more than you are, but it starts with being, with thinking, with habits of thought that are appropriate for the next level.

Got it? Looking at it another way, first, you need to be who you intend to become.

By the way, you are doing it already anyway, subconsciously. Think about that. You are already being who you will become.

So shape who you need to become with determination, forcefully, do the hard things, make the hard choices.

And right now, what you will become is being formed to a very large degree by the culture, for better or worse. And for who you desire to become, the culture may be forming you for the worse. Why?

Culture by definition is of the masses. It is geared toward the average, the mediocre.

Do you just want to be mediocre? The interesting thing about culture and being mediocre is that it is easy to market to.

Marketers and their statisticians who help them design advertising, movies, television, clothing, entertainment, and every type of item sold to consumers love culture, love averages.

They do not like outliers on the statistical curves, those points on the chart that are not lumped with the average. They cannot predict the behavior of outliers.

Successful people are *outliers*. By definition they are outliers, because they separate themselves from the masses, the average.

In some sense, they are in the culture that surrounds them, but they are not of the culture, so to speak. They have stepped aside from it just a bit. They know and see the culture for what it is. They see the way they are being marketed to, but like a fish that ignores the bait, they do not take the bait of the marketers or the culture of mediocrity.

IMHO, our culture is always wrong for those who want to achieve uncommon success. If it is the popular culture, it is wrong. Why? Because culture is of the masses. It is not geared to success, only to the average, to the mediocre. And it is always wrong because it caters to the lowest levels of behavior, making what was unacceptable yesterday acceptable today. The popular culture is about following the path of least resistance.

You are capable of far more than you are achieving now or even think you can achieve. You know this truth within yourself. Did you give 110% yesterday? How about the day before? How about today? Were you pushed to the limits? Did you push yourself to the limits?

If you want to achieve your aspirations, tap the full measure of potential within you, then you have to be today who you will become.

I suspect that you are asking, "OK, so how do I do that professor?"

Separating yourself from the masses is a matter of small decisions and habits of thought. It means thinking differently, doing the things that the average either overlook or are too lazy to do.

One of those is a simple outlook, a way of approaching things summarized as follows:

DO 27 NOT 25!™

"Huh, professor?"

Let me explain with a simple metaphorical example or story. Suppose that you are conscious of your health and exercise and do sit-ups or push-ups every day. Everyone in your class is doing twenty five sit-ups this week. Do not set your goal at twenty-five sit-ups like the rest of your classmates. And do not do just twenty-six, which is just one more, just a little above average.

Do twenty-seven instead, to push yourself beyond what you thought you could do or what anyone else would normally do. Do 27 not 25. You get the idea. Do not stop at 50, do 52. Do not stop at 105, do 107. Get it?

This applies to every endeavor, every area of your life. When you hit your goal, do not stop. Go further. Not just a little further, but one more push over a little further. No matter what it is, from studying, to cleaning, to exercising, to helping someone in need, to contributing to the club you are in. It is an attitude, a way of being.

One other thing. Every week, or month, increase it by five. It takes just a few seconds more. And you keep expanding your *margin of excellence*, not stopping at the average or above average. Always stay above those standards, in everything, in every area of your life.

Actually, this one thing is so powerful that if you applied it to everything you do in life without exception, every day, you would not need to keep reading. This one thing could alone change your life beyond your wildest dreams.

DO 27 NOT 25!

Always do more than average and always more than above average. You will fail, of course. That is the price you pay for trying, for success. Try just like Babe Ruth (the former baseball home run king, who also held the strike out record or more recently, Barry Bonds), Michael Jordan (the former basketball goal record and missed field goal record, now Kareem Abdul-Jabbar), Abraham Lincoln (who lost more elections than he won), and Thomas Edison (who had more than ten-thousand failed experiments before successfully inventing the light bulb). The founders of Macy's and KFC (Kentucky Fried Chicken) and so many more well-known successful people have the same story.

Successes often lose more than they win on the way to becoming successes.

When others see you fail, some will be supportive, some will be critical. But the decision to try for success is yours and yours alone. Do not listen to others around you as you make decisions for your future, to change and improve, to break bad habits, to excel, and to become what you dream. See Appendix D for someone I know who was both a spectacular failure and a spectacular success.

You will run into resistance when you start to change, for sure, so expect it. It will start with you, but you will get resistance from others as well. The inertia of your present habits will keep wanting to drag you back into your old habits of thinking and acting. It is the purpose and firm resolve to adopt the new ways of thinking and behaving and then doing them over and over again, for at least thirty days that will cement them in place. Got that? Do the same new habit every day for at least thirty days and you will make it permanent. There is a lot of research behind that assertion to back it up.

So it is with your friends and the current social scene you are part of. They know the old you or at least the current you, not the new you that you are trying to become. The 'new' you will likely be a threat to their sense of comfort with their own mediocrity. If you worry about what your peers think of you, the battle is lost before you begin. Not that you need to abandon your friends, but expect that your true friends will stick with you and encourage you. The rest are not true friends and you will find new friends as you grow and mature.

BTW, true friends do not know social status, so be careful to not get sucked into the self-serving and egotistical ways of thinking that only make friends by social status. True friends exhibit a love for the other that encourages the other to the best version of themselves as Matthew Kelly says.

Some social scenes are not good for where you are headed and some will support the changes you need to make. Be wise and very, very selective about who you associate with. I am not talking about snobbery here. I am talking about people with big hearts, minds and goals who want to have a lasting positive legacy. Maybe that is the association, temple, not-for-profit, synagogue, service organization, church or civic group instead of the "in" party group you've been invited to.

Friends and family know you a certain way. Some will unintentionally want to keep you there. They will not want you to change and be someone they do not know. They know you as you are. If you change you will be something unfamiliar to them, particularly if you decide to break some familiar cycle or pattern. That last one is a very big one, right?

Determine that you will not stay in the same rut, the same old patterns of thinking and behavior. Caution is needed here: listen to wisdom that will guide you on the path you have chosen. But don't seek wisdom from fools or the ignorant.

You are what you eat. You already know that. That's why you make certain choices about what you eat. Same with what you take into your head and heart.

Where is the finest computer in the world? Between your left ear and your right ear, of course. How are you programming it? What goes in your eyes and your ears resides in your mind and your heart. What comes forth from the mind and the heart in words and actions is the result of what you placed there.

Wow! Think about that one. What others hear and see coming from you is what you placed in your mind and heart, either intentionally or unintentionally.

What are you placing there intentionally?

College prepares you for a career. You will interact with customers, vendors, your employees, peers, and management.

They will come to know what you placed in the mind and the heart, either by default or by intent.

They will know your habits of thought.

They all deserve only the best from you, the most noble, the most sensitive, the most honest part of you, as well as your truth, wisdom, sincerity, love, and patience.

DO 27 NOT 25!

Make a decision to put the right stuff in your heart and mind and cut out the bad and negative stuff. Develop the right habits of thought. After all:

MY DESTINY IS HOT!

Yes, yes it is! Your destiny *is* your habits of thought! Decide today on your intentional habits of thought. Make your destiny your I-HOT!

DO 27 NOT 25: HOT POINT 1

Your destiny is determined by who you are. Who you are, at its core, is the habits of thought that come from what was placed in your head and heart. You alone choose what is placed there.

1. What are you placing in your head and heart by intent, your I-Hot?

2. What are you placing there by default, without intent (what culture dominates)?

3. Does that need to change to better match your dreams? How does that *specifically* need to change?

4. What decisions do you need to make to put the right things there by intent?

5. Are you programming yourself for those results?

Do 27 Not 25 HOT Point Resolution. I need to apply HOT Point 1, Do 27 Not 25, to the following areas of my life:

WEEK 2:

WHAT'S EVEN MORE IMPORTANT THAN YOUR EDUCATION?

Attitude

The longer I live, the more I realize the impact of attitude on life.

It is more important than the past, than education, than money, than circumstances, than failures, than success, than what other people think or say or do.

It is more important than appearance, giftedness, or skill.

The remarkable thing is—we have a choice every day of our lives regarding the attitude we embrace for that day.

We cannot change our past. We cannot change the fact that people will act in a certain way. We cannot change the inevitable.

The only thing we can do is play on the one string we have, and that is our attitude.

> *I am convinced that life is 10% what happens to me, and 90% how I react to it. And so it is with you. We are in charge of our attitudes.*
>
> —Chuck Swindoll

"Gee professor, I guess I never really thought about this one. My whole deal is on how I dress and look. That's important to me, you know?"

I get that. You are checking in as having a pulse! You are normal.

But, as we said in Week 1, your habits of thought result in your destiny. You are what you eat. You become what you think and how you think.

You are what you expect to become. That means your attitude about yourself, others, and everything around you.

So what is your overall attitude? Is it positive or negative? Optimistic or pessimistic? "Can do" or defeatist? Joyful or dour? Enthusiastic or depressive?

What attitude did you wake up with today? Did you make a decision about what your attitude would be or did you just let it happen to you?

Really? Why?

You mean to tell me that you let your attitude just be whatever you woke up with?

If you are in control of your attitudes, when will you exert control? How will you go about it daily? In everything you do including your attitude about life, you can make an active decision. Or not. You control that.

Not making a decision is a decision. Letting life happen to you, including how you program yourself and your attitude, is making a decision. The very essence of your humanity, your personhood, is in making decisions, not in relinquishing your responsibility to do so. Yes or no?

What will it be for you?

What attitude did you start the day with? Did it change? Why did it change? Did you let it happen to you or did you determine what your attitude would be?

Who is in control of your attitude? Is it you and your will power or is it your emotions and your environment? Really?

You can change your attitude about anything but you can never change another person. Ever. You are only in charge of your own attitudes.

The biggest fallacy there is, is thinking like this: "If I marry him or her, if I date him or her, if I live with him or her, party with him or her, and on and on, *then* they will change."

Not! No! Never!

People do not change unless they want to change. People change because they want whatever the change gets them more than what their present condition is getting them. And that is true especially of attitudes.

People will change their attitudes when the new attitudes get them more than what their current attitudes get them.

However, people will not change their attitudes easily. They tend to resist change and hold on in their insecurity until they see overwhelming evidence for a need to change. Then, when they finally do change, they often wonder why they took so long to change.

As your attitudes begin to change, as you begin to make more decisions about what you want from your life, you will discover that some people are toxic. They are not good for you. As a matter of fact, they are bad for you.

You will have to make some tough decisions about how much you want to associate with them. You must always act with charity and wisdom, of course. But be wise.

What has happened to you in the past, you cannot change. It just contributes to that rich mosaic that is you. Celebrate it and come to peace with it. Everyone, without exception, has burdens in life. It comes with being human.

But you cannot let your past dictate your future! You, and only you, can decide what your attitude is going to be now, today, and tomorrow.

Whatever the past is, be grateful for it. It is part of who you are today. If you have a lot to overcome, that can only be good for the fabric of your humanity. In a sense, the more you have to overcome, the better, because it will build your will-power muscles. Agreed?

Decide today who and what you will be. It cannot be what you were before. And it cannot be what you are today.

The opportunities you will have tomorrow await who you need to become starting today.

It requires an attitude that only you can control and decide on.

OK, so how do you do that, how do you start deciding on your attitude?

There is a very important principle here. It is called:

GUARD THE FIRST MINUTES OF CONSCIOUSNESS

"Say what, professor?"

The first minutes of consciousness when you wake up are the most important minutes of your life, of your day. Guard them like precious jewels. Let nothing get in the way, no matter where you are or what is going on within you or around you.

They are more important than music, television, texting, email, talking to friends, romance, computers, studying, sleeping, eating, or anything else you could possibly be doing.

Those first minutes form your consciousness, your attitudes for the day. They determine whether you decide on your attitudes or just let them happen to you. Protect that time with yourself and your inner thoughts in complete silence. Complete silence as soon as you wake up.

The principle here is to take at least the first five minutes of your day to make conscious decisions about your attitude, your disposition for the day, and what your response will be as it comes at you. You can make those decisions immediately.

GUARD THE FIRST MINUTES OF CONSCIOUSNESS

You can wake up and let life happen to you, which is what the vast majority of people do, what the average person does.

Or you can make a decision to be grateful, to be of service to others, to go above and beyond, to excel, to "Do 27 Not 25!" for the whole day.

The people who achieve their potential in life make those decisions for the day. They choose their attitudes. It is a success habit.

So you can spend the first minutes of your day doing it, or wake up five minutes early to do the same. Over time, you will find that five minutes is not long enough and you will want to take longer and longer.

I now guard the first one to two hours every morning, without fail, no matter where I am in the world, no matter the circumstances of my life. It is extremely rare that I miss a day. It has become a necessity in my life, more important than anything else I do.

There is a huge difference in how you interact with the world around you if you do this. It is a subtlety that the vast majority of people miss.

Will you be a person who reacts to life and the world as it comes to you, essentially going with the flow? Or will you be responsible for your personhood, make the decision, and act rather than react? You cannot control what life throws at you. But you can control who you are and how you respond based on your earlier decisions.

One more thing. After you guard the first five minutes of consciousness, spend another five minutes programming that brain of yours. Find something short and pointed that is positive and uplifting to the soul to read. After you have made an active attitude decision, then put something positive in your heart and brain.

Throughout the day, avoid the negative, which is all around you. Cut the negative news, information, entertainment, and influences out of your life. Run from all that is degrading of you or others. They are mind and heart pollution.

GUARD THE FIRST MINUTES OF CONSCIOUSNESS

Decide to take in only that which is uplifting to your mind and heart to the highest levels.

Then you will inspire others to do the same.

The world will be so much better for it.

DO 27 NOT 25: HOT POINT 2

The *First Minutes of Consciousness* is one of those little things that, when done over the course of time, can have a very large impact on your life, because it is out of the ordinary. It is extraordinary.

1. What do you need to do to have quiet solitude to guard the first minutes of consciousness each day?

2. What attitudes do you want to adopt for your day at this point? They can change over time and should change. Write down four or five attitudes.

3. What in your environment is not a good influence on the kinds of attitudes you want to adopt in your life? What can you do to eliminate or minimize those?

Do 27 Not 25 HOT Point Resolution. I will apply HOT Point 2, *Guard the First Minutes of Consciousness*, by deciding on these attitudes every morning:

WEEK 3:

WAIT! THE PURPOSE OF LIFE IS NOT HAPPINESS?

The Purpose of Life

I cannot believe that the purpose of life is to be "happy."
I think the purpose of life is to be useful, to be responsible, to be compassionate.
It is, above all, to matter, to count, to stand for something, to have made some difference that you lived at all.

—Leo Rosten

"Hey, man, wait! Are you crazy? Of course I want to be happy! What are you talking about? If I am not happy then life is a drag. I have some old guy trying to tell me not to be happy? Get real and get lost, professor!"

I know. But wait...

Notice that *happy* is in quotes. I think he means that *being happy* can't be the singular focus you live your life for.

Try this: the singular focus on being happy equals self-gratification, which is self-focused. That excludes a lot: being a superb leader and manager, effective parenting, serving your country, helping the less fortunate, and helping teammates, for example. Those require a focus on the other.

Happiness in the now is what our culture today is all about. It is all about doing what makes us happy for the moment, what feels good. Nearly all the messages you see and hear in the media are focused on being happy by having this or that pleasure. Do it now; no rules is the rule!

That happiness is fleeting. Like a drug. Then you need more and more. People become narcissistic (vain, focused on feeling good) in their search for more of what makes them happy, what brings them pleasure in the moment.

We have freedom, yes. To pursue happiness, yes. To pursue life, liberty, and happiness, as it is enshrined in the United States' founding documents for those of you who live in the US or are familiar with the US Declaration of Independence.

That is not the freedom to do whatever we damn well want, when we want, how we want, where we want. That is chaos and anarchy. It is a form of slavery to passion, emotion, and immaturity.

Freedom entails a responsibility to contribute to others, to country, to work, to our families, and to our communities in a moral fashion. Your contributions to the good of others can only be valid if they are done with the highest moral and ethical standards that you are aware of. It is never acceptable to claim to achieve a moral end by doing something unethical or immoral. No Robin Hoods allowed!

To quote the philosopher Karol Wojtyla:

> True freedom is not advanced in the permissive society, which confuses freedom with license to do anything whatever and which in the name of freedom proclaims a kind of general amorality. It is a caricature (distortion) of freedom to claim that people are free to organize their lives with no reference to moral values, and to say that society does not have to ensure the protection and advancement of ethical values. Such an attitude is destructive of freedom and peace.

Kinda high-minded wording, huh? You have to read it a few times to get it. But you get it, right? Amoral or immoral license is not the same as freedom. In fact, it is the opposite because it is destructive of true freedom and peace. They are at war, figuratively and literally, with each other.

If your focus is on life, liberty, and the pursuit of happiness, then that is the pursuit of the fulfillment of the human potential, the growth of your personhood.

It is expressed in the climate of freedom and peace and guarded by the highest moral and ethical standards you know.

The fulfillment of your human potential, paradoxically, is best done by a focus on others. I don't mean the toxic people-pleasing of the adult children of alcoholics (ACOA, check it out sometime). The majority of the population exhibits the dysfunctional symptoms of adult children of "...aholics" of some type. But it is getting your eyes off yourself and focusing on the service of others that is the key to the fulfillment you so much desire. Wow!

The surprising reality is that for you to fulfill your human potential, your focus on the good of others will be the most powerful thing you can do. It calls forth from every part of your humanity that which will be the most powerful in developing the fullness of your humanity and potential.

What's the old saying, "It is in giving that you receive?" I know you get it. Simple, countercultural and always true. In season, and out of season, if you know what I mean.

It is in having counted for something, having mattered, having made a difference, that brings you joy. That joy cannot be taken from you, even when your emotions tell you that you are not "happy" at the moment. It is completely possible to be joyful, even if you are not happy, and in fact, can be enduring some suffering at the moment. Think of a very tired mom, bathing a child, who may not be 'happy' at the moment, but is joyful for her privilege of being a mom to this child. True joy.

Joy comes from meaningful service, from fulfillment of your human potential in doing it. And in that way, your legacy becomes bigger than you. Hear that? It becomes bigger than you!

Joy and fulfillment comes from the focus of parents on children, workers on teammates, peers on customers, teachers on students, soldiers on the mission, public servants on the community and nation.

Don't worry about focusing on yourself to take care of yourself. Unless you are an ACOA (adult child of an alcoholics) or something, you have developed that skill well enough. You can easily take care of yourself.

For me, if I never look out for myself again for the rest of my life, I will have spent too much time doing it. I have that skill down pat. I can do that without thinking!

But to be conscious of the needs of others, that is a different story. Develop within you a constant and conscious drive to:

FOCUS ON THE NEEDS OF OTHERS

Curiously, that is what makes a good athlete, a good club member or leader, a good study team member, or a good classmate. Making those around you successful by what you do makes you successful.

Now is the time to make a fundamental decision about your purpose in life, how you will have counted, what you will have stood for. That always is measured by your impact on others.

As Rick Warren, the author of *The Purpose Driven Life* says, "It is not about you!" It's a good book and worth reading, no matter what your affiliation is. Actually it is better than good, it is powerful in helping to change one's focus.

The decision to think that way needs to be done now if you want to make it a habit. Start practicing that skill now. Not later. Make it a habit now.

Why? Because it takes a long time to develop a good habit and a long time to kill bad ones. And the way you kill bad habits is by replacing them with good habits. Get that? Build new habits to replace bad habits.

When you enter that first full-time job with your college education in hand, what will be the first impressions people have of you? It is too late to decide that then. It needs to be decided now.

Be what you need to be, starting now. Not later. Remember, you are waking up early and taking time to reflect on your thoughts, your attitudes. Include time to think about your focus on others.

This is the stuff heroes are made of, in families, at work, in service, in religious organizations, in communities, and in nations.

We do not need more self-focused politicians, community leaders, and business people. We have enough of those already. What we need are heroic people in all walks of life.

You were made to be a hero in whatever you choose to do in life, however simple that may look to others. Be it. Start today, not tomorrow.

FOCUS ON THE NEEDS OF OTHERS

Decide now to do it. Decide now what your purpose in life is, what your legacy will be.

> How will you count for something?
> Grab the vision of it and go for it.
> The ride is exhilarating!

DO 27 NOT 25 : HOT POINT 3

When you think back, you can remember times when you said something or did something that made a positive impact on someone else's life. They may have thanked you or not, but you felt good about having done it. Remember?

1. What are some of the things you have done in life that have brought you joy (but maybe not happiness, at the time)?

2. What things bring you joy at this point in your life?

3. What are the big picture things (your dreams) you want to do with your life that will count for something, that will make a difference in the world?

4. In what ways do you see the connection between those things and the fulfillment of your potential? Between those things and joy?

Do 27 Not 25 HOT Point Resolution. I will apply HOT Point 3, *Focus on the needs of others,* **by looking for opportunities to put it into practice in these circumstances:**

WEEK 4:

NEW WAYS TO REALLY BELIEVE IN YOU!

Believing In Yourself

standing for what you believe in
regardless of the odds against you
and the pressure that tears at your resistance
means courage

keeping a smile on your face
when inside you feel like dying
for the sake of supporting others
means strength

stopping at nothing
and doing what in your heart
you know is right
means determination

doing more than is expected
to make another's life a little more bearable
without uttering a single complaint
means compassion

> helping a friend in need
> no matter the time or effort
> to the best of your ability
> means loyalty
>
> giving more than you have
> and expecting nothing
> in return
> means selflessness
>
> holding your head high
> and being the best you know you can be
> when life seems to fall apart at your feet
> and facing each difficulty with
> the confidence that time will bring
> you better tomorrows
> and never giving up
> means believing in yourself…
>
> —Mary Ellen Joseph

"Hey, professor, that is one powerful poem! Wow! I had to read that a second time to get it. I was just thinking about what it says and…Wait, someone just knocked on the door, *pizza guy*.…. OK, where were we? Oh, yeah. Well, I just graduated from high school and you want to talk to me about grown up stuff like this? That's for later. Get a life man! I am here to P-A-R-T-Y!"

Oh, sorry. For a minute there it seemed like you really got it.

One quick question before you go, BTW. Just when were you thinking you might get around to growing up?

Just bustin' on ya, OK? Lighten up! Hang in there with me a minute.

You graduated from high school. You are in college for only a few years. Finally in college. Yay! You never thought it would come, that it could not get here fast enough. You could not wait to get out of there and be on your own.

And you are still on the high, loving it at this point in the semester, as it should be. Congratulate yourself for your accomplishment.

So now you have started your intellectual development in preparation for your career in a few years. And some growth will come from that alone.

But not enough for you to be the success you want to be, to be exceptional. You already have said *no* to being a failure and to being just mediocre, to just being average.

Guess what? You have much more potential than you even know.

What does it take to push the limits of your potential? First, you need a greater level of maturity than you have had in the past or have at the moment. A greater level of maturity than the average, than the culture encourages.

So this isn't high school. We have already talked about beginning to think, act and be what you need to be for your career. Your intellectual development needs to match what is going on in your head and heart so that your preparation is balanced. Guess which one has the greater impact on your success and your destiny? (Hint: it is not your grades!)

You cannot stay at the same level of maturity and development.

Now, back to the grownup stuff and where you were before the pizza guy knocked at the door and distracted you.

That poem had some pretty powerful words, huh? Those are some pretty awesome traits to have as a person: courage, strength, determination, compassion, loyalty, and selflessness. Well, do you have those? Of course you do to some extent, most likely.

The question is, what are you doing to develop those in yourself? Some of them you are better at than others. Which ones? And some really need a lot of work. What are you doing about it?

Those noble traits or virtues are part of a person's character. They do not favor education, intelligence, wealth, race, age, sex, or anything else.

They can be possessed by anyone who wants them badly enough to pursue them. And the character of a person who possesses them to a large degree makes that person a leader, an influential person, no matter what they are doing in life.

People are naturally drawn to those who exhibit those traits or virtues because they exude goodness. Effective leaders in any industry or career exhibit those.

People who exhibit those traits inspire others. They inspire others to be more than they are. They inspire them to imitate those virtues.

Do you want to be influential so you can have a positive impact? Of course you do!

Then consider how you want to go about developing those noble traits, those virtues within yourself. You do not need anyone's permission—except your own. All you need is the belief that you can do it.

You can choose to develop those traits: courage, strength, determination, compassion, loyalty, and selflessness. What does it require? You have to:

CHOOSE BELIEF IN YOURSELF!

At this point in the semester, are you waking up early and spending the first part of your day making those decisions about your attitudes?

Are you reading something positive, something that directs your habits of thought toward the destiny you have chosen? Are you making a daily decision to do so, to choose your attitude for the day, no matter how you feel or what you anticipate for the day in front of you?

The question is, do you believe in yourself enough to do this? And if you already think you are on the right track, can you go the extra 10 percent, do the extra sit-ups, so to speak? Can you *Do 27 not 25* by developing those traits within you?

Those who are successful on their own terms (not someone else's) separate themselves by distinguishing themselves from the masses, from the culture.

Did you make the 110% decision today this poem talks about? Did you decide to do twenty-seven sit-ups instead of twenty-five? Give your homework the extra 10 percent? Go the extra mile for someone else? Go above and beyond the call of duty to serve in the organization you belong to at school?

All of this disposition trains you to do what counts, when it counts. It trains you to act with strength and courage, no matter how you feel, for the good of others, reaching down inside to be heroic, quietly and without notice, in your own way. As a matter of fact, doing it without notice is better for your character development, so avoid looking for accolades.

The effect, because it is so countercultural, has a huge impact on the development of your character. It goes beyond anything you can possibly comprehend right now.

That training, those habits of thought, and those actions that shape your destiny (in your career and life) require a choice on your part. They will form who you will be.

The curious thing is, your thoughts and actions shape your destiny, regardless of what you are doing right now. The difference is a *choice*. The end result years down the road will be hugely different depending on the small choices you make now.

So choose carefully. Choose now.

CHOOSE BELIEF IN YOURSELF!

A bright future awaits those who steer their lives toward a bright future.

Yes, there will be difficulties and storms on the ocean of life, especially in this culture. But like a wise captain, you can chart a course toward your goal and steer your ship toward it.

Full steam ahead!

Aye, aye, captain, full steam ahead! On course!

DO 27 NOT 25 : HOT POINT 4

Life is pretty busy in college right about now, with studies, clubs, parties, dating, internships, and working part-time perhaps. Trying to focus on this kind of stuff can feel like overload unless you find a way to make it flow naturally in your life. The first few minutes of the day are the secret to letting it just unfold in your life.

1. Describe some examples, some instances, of when you have exhibited some of those traits, those virtues (selflessness, courage, and so on) in your life. This is really important!

2. How did it make you feel in those instances?

3. Which of those virtues do you think you need to work on the most?

4. How can you go about developing the virtues that are your weakest ones?

5. And how can you reinforce those that are your strongest traits?

Do 27 Not 25 HOT Point Resolution. I will work on developing HOT Point 4, *Choose belief in yourself,* **virtues by doing the following immediately:**

WEEK 5:

YOUR REAL JOB DESCRIPTION: NOT WHAT YOU THINK IT IS

MY JOB DESCRIPTION

My job is to be the best I can at what I do. Not just "good" or "good enough." Use my best judgment. Produce my best quality.

My job is to be a team player and help out where the need is greatest. Get out of my protective little world. Be flexible.

My job is to make each hour effective. Wasted time is not recoverable and wasting it is inexcusable.

My job is to continuously improve. Try to do everything I do today better than I did yesterday. Take initiative.

My job is to enjoy the time I have. Life is short. If I don't enjoy what I'm doing then I am doing the wrong thing. Make a change.

My job is to learn something new every day. Learn from my mistakes and successes as well as from those of others.

My job is to urge and encourage everyone else to do their job. We will only reach our full potential if everyone is involved.
My job is to think. Doing it right the first time is much better than doing it over. Sure, it is work, but thinking for myself is better than the alternative.
My job is to treat everyone with dignity and respect. I need to build relationships that value everyone, no matter who, equally.
My job is to be part of the solution, not part of the problem. Look for ways to solve problems before they get blown out of proportion.
My job is to get into my customers' shoes. Think about how they feel. I need to remember that I have internal as well as external customers.
My job is to make us a world class company. The benefits of this are the stability and growth of our company and of us as individuals.

—Gary R. Packard

"Hey professor, this is a little early isn't it? I am a long way from having a full-time job. I am just a college student up to my eyeballs in study and work!"

Yeah, I know. But stop just a minute. Look up from your work. Smell the roses a minute, will you? The point is, you do plan on graduating, right? And getting a real job, right?

YOUR REAL JOB DESCRIPTION: NOT WHAT YOU THINK IT IS

Well, then how about just stopping long enough to think about what that job is going to demand of you so that all this hard work will pay off. This hard work you are doing right now can have some meaning in unusual ways you may not have thought about before.

Practicing that job description as a college student will make you a better student and develop those traits for when you enter the world of work. That will put you ahead of 98 percent of your peers.

We have talked in the last four weeks about the foundations of a successful career.

Getting a 4.0 grade point average is not sufficient, but it helps. Good grades, earned honestly—note the caveat of *honestly*—are not so much a measure of intelligence as hard work, determination, will power, and attitude. Apply these principles and you can get better grades than you ever thought possible, because you are giving it more focused effort than you ever have.

Just a note on honesty. It is always a good quality to live by, for yourself and for others, of course. Yet I see people lying, cheating, and stealing. At times we have all failed in those areas, right? None of us is guiltless. But we are all capable of avoiding those vices. Many however, are complacent when it comes to those vices. They go along with the culture of mediocrity and rationalize it by saying, "Everyone is doing it." I feel sad for them.

Why do I feel sad for them and not a moral outrage? I do feel outrage, of course, but the sadness is dominant.

It is because besides the fact that it is illegal or against the rules to lie, lying, cheating or stealing will catch up with them at some point. And who do they think they are cheating? They think it is the system. But who are they really cheating? Why of course, you and me and everyone else! We pay for their moral corruption.

But worse than that, they are cheating themselves in the most insidious way. It is bad for their self-esteem. It is bad psychologically. The "accuser" sits there in the back of their head. That little voice says, "See, you are no good. You can't do it honestly. You are not as smart as the rest so you cheat to look good. You are not a good student." And on and on it goes.

The eventual fruit of lying, cheating or stealing is lowered self-esteem and self-worth no matter how artfully it is disguised. I have run into so many people who look great on the outside from what you can observe, but are hollow and filled with pain and low self-esteem on the inside because of their unethical behaviors in the past and present.

Actually, success in education, like success in your career, is as much about your attitude as anything. It is all in how you approach the tasks at hand. We have already talked about how important attitude is.

Much of this job description applies to you now, as a college student. When will you choose to excel in your job and career? When you graduate? The day after you start work?

YOUR REAL JOB DESCRIPTION: NOT WHAT YOU THINK IT IS

Maybe you think you are planning on it now. But have you made all the decisions to excel that back up your plan to be a success? If so, are you practicing those habits now?

If you have not "bellied up to the bar," as the saying goes, and made those decisions and started practicing those habits, when were you planning on doing it? Graduation is too late.

Practice being all those things that will lead to excellence now.

Practice right now.

Don't wait to start tomorrow for fear of putting it off again. And again. And again. And ending up in unintended and undecided mediocrity. That's a decision you make now, at this very moment.

"I am above that professor! I know I will be a success!" In the words of Shakespeare: "Thou dost protest too much!"

Are you totally committed to everything in the job description and are you practicing all those right now? Are you resisting all the temptations to go with the culture even now, in the current environment in college? Then good for you!

But if you are human like the rest of us, while we hope to be successful, we have these little areas of self-indulgence, laziness, or procrastination that measure up to less than the standard of excellence this points to.

So what needs to change in your habits of thought, your attitudes, your actions and activities, your behaviors, and your character?

Here is where the ACOA, Alcoholics Anonymous twelve-step program can be very valuable. Step four is to take a *fearless inventory*. In their case, it means a fearless *moral* inventory. But this is not AA or ACOA. Doing that step is not bad, and as a matter of fact, I highly recommend it. I suggest you get a copy and do the ACOA version of the twelve steps, in particular step four.

In this case, it is a fearless inventory of habits of thought, attitudes, actions, activities, behaviors, and character. Figure out what needs to change. Make a list and determine what they are and how you need to change.

By the way, others might even give you a clue. Your defects are a secret only to you. Think about that. Funny, huh? LOL! I laugh at myself every time I think about that. What am I hiding from, anyway? The truth about myself?

Everyone else in your life knows what your defects and weaknesses are. Just ask them. Don't worry about your self-esteem here. You need the information in all candor and truth to work on your game. That's why you hire a coach, right? In this case, this book is the coach. (And for those who are really serious, I do group and on rare occasions, one-on-one coaching. Contact me on the web site if you are interested.)

So get the information any way you can. And use that information to your benefit. Make a list of your defects and the actions you can take to implement change, starting now.

That is forming another extraordinarily powerful characteristic in you:

ADOPT AN ATTITUDE OF CONTINUOUS IMPROVEMENT

It is a well-known business principle, the characteristic of continuous quality improvement which makes for excellent companies.

But it also applies to self-improvement in every area of your life, intellectually, physically, relationally, emotionally, and spiritually. Whatever you did yesterday is not good enough for today. No resting on laurels.

And here is the curious thing: if you do not have an attitude of continuous improvement, the only other possible choice is staying the same. In other terms, that is called complacency, and that is a very dangerous place to be, because complacency resists change.

In every aspect of life, you either change and improve or succumb to the forces around you. In a competitive world, that is not where you want to be. And in life in general, the whole world is changing, so complacency is dangerous in all aspects of life.

In the parts of your world that are not competitive, namely your relationships, emotions, spiritual, physical and intellectual, it is even more critical. Why? Because each of those is changing and one is either growing or stagnating. And if one stagnates, you wither on the vine, drying up and becoming useless to yourself and everyone else.

People need you to change and grow. Everyone around you needs that from you.

These things practiced consistently will make you stand out from the crowd. And that is what people on your teams and those who work for and with you are depending on you to do.

But you cannot stop with that. If you want success in your life you need to grow beyond what you need to be for where you are now. In the case of a job, you want to grow beyond the requirements of the position you have.

But the same thing applies in the rest of your life. If you are a new mom or dad, good for you, but be ready to be a parent of a toddler before you need to be.

Note the attitudes that are embedded in the job description. And notice those that are not included: negativity, sarcasm, cynicism, mediocrity, and indifference.

Wherever and whenever they encounter those attitudes, those traits, wise people will take whatever measures are necessary to get them out of their lives. Those negative traits will never contribute to your success. Ever. And those attitudes are never justified under any circumstance. Ever. Resolve to eliminate even the slightest amount of those from your life. They are destructive.

Those positive attitudes that are embedded in the job description are the attitudes that are absolutely key to your success. The job market is competitive and getting more so. It will not get less so or easier.

ADOPT AN ATTITUDE OF CONTINUOUS IMPROVEMENT

Your competitive advantage for your career and life needs to be built now. You cannot wait until you graduate to acquire these attributes of character. Then all those characteristics will affect all that you do now and in the next few years, which will affect how you perform. And that will affect your reputation, the recommendations you get, and your ability to direct your life and career in the directions you want it to go.

Make a habit of self-examination daily. Do not accept what you did today as good enough for tomorrow. No complacency here, right?

That shortcoming or failure you had today? Learn from it and then forget it. Don't dwell on it. Move on. Resolve to improve. Make amends, forgive. Let go. Refocus.

Rise to the next level in each area of your life.

Rise up to greater heights!

DO 27 NOT 25 : HOT POINT 5

Up to this point you may not have really thought that much about what a real job would demand. The idea of being a little bit better every day in every area of your life may be new perhaps. But to adopt an attitude of continuous improvement in all areas of life and formalize that attitude into conscious decisions and actions is now your objective.

1. When you look at the list in the job description, which of those are areas of strength for you? Which come naturally to you?

2. Which of those are either ones you need to work on improving or need to develop because you have not really thought about them?

3. What are the areas of your life where you can really apply the attitude of continuous improvement?

Do 27 Not 25 HOT Point Resolution. I will apply HOT Point 5, *Adopt an attitude of continuous improvement*, in the areas of life I identified above in these specific ways:

WEEK 6:

THE BOTTOM LINE: NO ONE OWES YOU ANYTHING! GO FOR IT!

The Bottom Line
Nobody owes you a living.
What we achieve or fail to achieve in our lifetime
is directly related to the choices we make.
We don't choose our parents or childhood,
but we can choose our own direction.
Everyone has problems and obstacles to overcome,
but that too is relative to each individual.
Nothing is carved in stone,
we can change almost anything in our life
if we want to badly enough.
Losers make excuses.
Those who take responsibility for their actions
are the real winners in life.
They meet life's challenges head on,
knowing there are no guarantees,
and give it all they've got.
It's never too late or too early to begin.

> **For time plays no favorites
> and will pass whether we act or not.
> So take control of your life,
> Dare to dream and take risks...
> If you aren't willing to work for your goals
> Don't expect others to.
> Believe in yourself and
> compete for the life you want.**
>
> —Anonymous

"Hey, professor! This is kind of in-your-face. I mean really! There are excuses, right professor?"

Not really, my friend. You know the old saying about the homework or project or whatever: "I didn't have time."

Is that for real? Or rather, did you just not make the time? Whatever it was, you had some other higher priority. You did not make the time. No excuse. That's the plain and simple truth. See how that works? That is taking responsibility for your actions.

Where I went to school, there were only three acceptable answers to a question: "Yes sir," "No sir," or "No excuse sir." Plain and simple. Direct and to the point.

We have talked so far about some things, some habits of thought that are foundational to your future success, your life and career:

THE BOTTOM LINE: NO ONE OWES YOU ANYTHING! GO FOR IT!

1. Do 27 not 25!
2. Guard the first minutes of consciousness
3. Focus on the needs of others
4. Choose belief in yourself
5. Adopt an attitude of continuous improvement

Today you can set goals for yourself that are meaningful to you and go for them, no matter who you are, what you are, or where you are.

And you can do that, no matter what you have experienced or have had to overcome. Set your goals! Do you have a written set of goals? And a plan for achieving them? We will spend some time on that later, count on it.

One of the most powerful things you can do in your life is not just to have goals. It is to write them down and have a plan for achieving them.

And then go for them with everything you've got. And along the way:

MAKE NO EXCUSES!

Whatever you achieve or fail to achieve every single day, own it. There are no excuses. Just the reality of what you did and what you did not do. Plain and simple, take responsibility for your actions.

Now that is really different. We live in a blaming society with excuses for everything. Culture says to blame someone or something else for my lack of achievement, my lack of character, my failures, my lack of _____, you name it.

That breeds a certain "lameness of personhood." In fact, it gives over the person to outside forces so they are no longer responsible for themselves. In giving in to that temptation, they give up their individuality and uniqueness of their very nature as a human being, as people.

Stop for a moment. Consider carefully what I've just told you. Have you ever fallen into that trap? Can you think about an instance of having done that and its effects? Can you see it in others? It is an insidious disease infecting our culture today and it is very widespread. It breeds helplessness and that "lameness of the person" I talked about.

If you ever feel the temptation of an excuse coming on, RUN! Do not fall into the trap of defending yourself with an excuse. Take the reality of the situation like a man or woman.

MAKE NO EXCUSES!

The achievement of your full potential depends on it. Take full responsibility for your life in all its dimensions.

No one else can live your life for you. But that does not stop them from trying, either unintentionally, out of good intentions, or intentionally, demanding you live a life that suits them and their expectations of what you should be.

There is a saying, "Don't let people 'should' all over you!" Ha! Get it? Funny or what?

That is particularly true the closer the people are to you in your life. Emotional attachments are the worst when it comes to that.

Where does your happiness come from? If you allow it to come from others, it will fail you, and even hurt you, sometimes badly. Happiness comes from within you. You do not need anyone or anything else to make you happy. Find that place first and be there in yourself first.

Let me repeat that: you do not need anyone or anything else to make you happy.

I repeat again, *you do not need anyone or anything else to make you happy*, no matter how much you think you do. Not friends, not lovers, not money, not fame, not power, not position, and on and on.

Nothing in this world outside of you can make you happy for long. That comes from inside, from the soul, your very being. Look at all the unhappy people at every level of society; they have missed it. They think it comes from outside themselves.

Find that place of happiness that you own, on your own, so that there are no excuses for not having it and possessing it within yourself. Look deep within yourself to find it, to the core of your being, your very soul. And make no excuses for not possessing it. Only you can do that, no one else.

When you get there, people cannot possibly "should all over you." Their attempts at that, and the control that comes with that will not work.

Be wary of control. Control comes in many forms. Some people have no boundaries, and some do not respect the boundaries of others. They will try to control others, including you. And it works both ways because they allow others to control them.

No, you can be your own person.

I am not talking about rebelling against the various forms of legitimate authority. The rules and laws that give order to the conduct of society are needed, otherwise we would have anarchy and chaos. Rebellion against rightful and moral authority is just childishness, a type of immaturity. It's acting like a five-year-old.

So set goals in your life that are the fulfillment of your potential. Write them down. Plan them out. And then take on a no-excuses attitude, a can-do attitude.

You are the only one who can make your dreams a reality.

Set your goals, design your reality around the things that count, the things that make a difference in the world, the things that become your legacy.

MAKE NO EXCUSES!

Be idealistic. Someone has to for the good of the world and our culture. Look at those who did and the results of their idealistic beliefs and not accepting things as they were: Gandhi, Martin Luther King, Mother Teresa, Nelson Mandela, and on and on.

Be an idealist.

Then make no excuses in striving to accomplish those lofty goals.

The whole world awaits you!

DO 27 NOT 25 : HOT POINT 6

OK, so this one was a little tough. You have always lived having someone telling you what to do (or wished you would have had them around to do that). When you did not do what you needed to do, sometimes others, including parents, made excuses for you. Or you made excuses, right? It sounded something like, "Hey, the reason I am like this is…" or "The reason I did not do that was…" or "The reason I did that was…"

1. In what ways have you made excuses for yourself in the past?

2. How has the making of excuses for yourself hurt you as you look back on it?

3. Have you taken the time to write down the goals for your life? If you have not, write down some of them here now:

Do 27 Not 25 HOT Point Resolution. I am going to adopt HOT Point 6 *Make no excuses* **as an attitude for my future by doing the following:**

WEEK 7:

YOU KNOW A TREE BY ITS FRUITS

Golden Gems
A careless word may kindle strife;
A cruel word may wreck a life;
A bitter word may hate instill;
A brutal word may smite and kill;

A gracious word may smooth the way;
A joyous word may light the day;
A timely word may lessen stress;
A loving word may heal and bless.

—Anonymous

"OK, professor, basically I am a good person right now. Yeah, I know, sometimes I do those things at the top of the list, but not intentionally (mostly) and not all the time."

Well my friend, that is good to hear. I commend you. At this point I want to take a little bit of a different approach, so bear with me. I want to bring a new lesson to you and raise your awareness.

Last week, we talked about the bottom line:

- Living your own life

- Setting goals and going after what you want

- Taking responsibility for your actions

- Finding your happiness within yourself

- Making no excuses

You see, when it comes to setting goals and achieving them, what matters is not just setting your goals and overcoming obstacles.

What matters *even more* is how you get there. As you go, what do you leave in your wake? Like a boat cutting through the water, what do you leave in the wake behind you?

Do you leave damaged people and feelings in your wake? Resentment and hurt?

Or do people come away from every encounter encouraged, feeling good about the encounter, or at least satisfied that a good of some type was accomplished. Even in tough situations, the other person's dignity can be protected and they can come away uplifted, even if they sting from a correction, for instance.

Your words count because words have impact. They affect people's lives more that you can imagine in the long term.

You know how important words are. You have been on the receiving end of words that have had a positive effect and words that have had a negative effect. You have been lifted up by words and you have been cut down by words. Words have meaning and impact, sometimes for a very, very long time.

You are too young to appreciate it now because you have not lived long enough, but ask anyone a lot older than you how some particularly positive or negative words affected them for many, many years, even a whole lifetime.

Do you know that some people go through their whole lives being controlled by or reacting to words that were spoken to them as young children? That's why they are in therapy (or not, but maybe should be).

You are first known by your words and then by your actions.

Are you known as positive, upbeat, uplifting of others, caring, encouraging, and giving?

Or are you known as a nice person at best? Or as negative, harsh, critical, foul, sarcastic, or even worse? Are people motivated by you or demotivated and discouraged? Are you even aware of your impact?

You get the picture.

I once knew a guy in a big company I worked for who trashed his career over his foul jokes. Problem is, he did not know why he was never promoted, really. There is another issue there. While he thought he was funny around most people, there were enough who objected, including some customers, that it trashed his career. He insulted a lot of good people, both customers and coworkers, but he was oblivious to it! And oblivious to the feedback he was getting.

Same with another guy, who was very talented technically. But he was constantly negative and critical about everything around him, including the company. He talked people and organizations down. It killed his career. And it hurt a lot of his coworkers. He was so insensitive that he did not even realize the effect he was having on others.

A tree is known by its fruits.

BEAR GOOD FRUIT.

What is in your head and your heart is what comes out of your mouth as words and in your actions, the fruit of who you are.

It is not different than that. It could not be otherwise.

The words you use and your actions toward others will either be good fruit or bad fruit.

So that is why those first minutes of consciousness after you wake up are so important to make real, active decisions about what your attitude will be for the day.

They determine how you will conduct yourself no matter what is going on with you. What is going on within you is not relevant to others and your responsibilities toward them. Your responsibility to them is to give them the best of you. To

BEAR GOOD FRUIT

in everything you do, in all your responsibilities. Toss the bad fruit. It will only make you and others sick. It is poisonous to the world and the world does not need any more of that.

Look at the list in the poem and how it is grouped. The top four items are those that demean others. We all have fallen into those traps at times. We all fail at those. But that does not make it OK.

People who do those things, myself included, are thieves and robbers when we do that. We steal another's dignity and self-respect for our convenience or to make us feel good.

Who gave us the right to steal from another? What justification can we conjure up for such outrageous behavior? There is none. Under no circumstances is it OK to steal another's dignity, no matter what they have done.

The second four items are indicators of someone who is a giver, someone who is generous toward others. Someone who is a builder of people, families, organizations, and communities. Someone who does not count the cost of their giving, but gives to see the fruits of another blossom.

There can be no justification, ever, for being the robber and thief of someone's dignity, no matter how badly you have been treated or how badly someone has screwed up.

Never is it justified to call someone stupid or a jerk or any other slur. That starts with what parents say to children and extends to you and how you treat your coworkers, team members, and employees.

I cringe every time I hear a parent using demeaning words to their children. What a very sad thing to do! Children deserve only unconditional love, even when they are misbehaving. Firm discipline done in love without demeaning words are what a child needs in that case. It starts there and extends to everyone in our life.

You can go through the worst possible circumstances in a relationship without ever demeaning another or stealing their dignity. I know. It has happened to me. A number of times.

None of this precludes tough love, rules, or discipline. It does not preclude having to discipline someone or even fire them. But all that has to be done while preserving their dignity.

Decide today whether you will be a thief or a giver, a robber or a builder of people.

Then be it. Now. Today. Not tomorrow, because it will get put off.
Then in the morning decide again for tomorrow.

BEAR GOOD FRUIT

in your words and actions toward others.
Good fruit is appreciated by everyone.
The world needs your good fruit. Now.

DO 27 NOT 25 : HOT POINT 7

When it comes to the words people use, you know full well the impact they have on you. You remember. Your memories are filled with many things that were said to you. You remember some of the good things, the encouragements, but also the bad things, the hurtful things. Why is that? Because the human person remembers pain more vividly than pleasure.

1. When do you most often fall into the trap of doing those four things at the top of the list?

2. How does it feel to think of yourself in those instances as being a thief?

3. You know the joy of being a giver, of bearing good fruit, of doing the four things on the bottom of the list. How does it make you feel when you do those?

Do 27 Not 25 HOT Point Resolution. I will apply HOT Point 7, *Bear good fruit*, by looking for opportunities to put it into practice in these circumstances:

WEEK 8:

DARE MIGHTY THINGS—OR SNIVEL AND WHINE!

To Dare Mighty Things

**Far better it is to dare mighty things,
to win glorious triumphs even though checkered by failure,
than to rank with those poor spirits who neither enjoy much nor suffer much
because they live in the grey twilight that knows neither victory nor defeat.**

—Theodore Roosevelt

"Say what? Dare mighty things, professor? You gotta be kidding, right? I am just a college student trying to get a degree and have fun here. What's this have to do with college or my career?"

Funny you would ask that. Let me explain.

What is the meaning of the last part of that quote that begins "those poor spirits who?" Both the heights and depths of the human experience come from great effort expended on daring to achieve much.

There is nothing like achieving a goal that was a stretch or even thought to be impossible. There is nothing like the disappointment of failing to achieve it either. But both extremes are healthy and build the character of the person to their fullest.

The great danger to the full development of the human person is the mediocrity of our culture, which draws people into the trap of seeking the pleasures of the here and now instead of focusing on the longer term goals of achievement. It robs those it ensnares (the majority of the population) of the real richness that the human person is capable of experiencing.

You have a decision to make here and now in this moment: continue to get sucked in by the culture or dare to be different. Be a little apart from it and set lofty goals for yourself, stretching to live to your potential.

By now, you know that I am not talking about fame or power or money or position, but achieving the *extraordinary* in your vocation and station in life. That might mean becoming an extraordinary athlete, writer, painter, mother, father, friend, coworker, manager, leader, student, or whatever you believe your life calling is so that you can maximize the talents and gifts you have as a unique person.

An interesting point here. Do not try, as you set down your aspirations for your life, to be what you are not.

Let me say that again. Your happiness and joy in life will come from achieving the goals you have that are consistent with who you are, not with what someone else is or what someone else tells you that you need to be. Do not waste the time or endure the frustrations of trying to live someone else's dreams for you. Rather, put your heart into who you are, who you were uniquely created to be.

To do that requires that you take the time to write down who you are and what you want your life to be like. Have you taken the time to write down the twenty to thirty things that would describe what you would like your life to be like? Can you paint a word picture of it? Sure, it will change over time, but that is OK and normal.

If you have that word picture and it captures your heart and imagination, you will have an infinitely better chance of living it than if you never take the time to do it.

Does that word picture include relational things or just material things? Out of the thirty-six things that describe what I want my own life to be, only one, a house with a big yard, is material. The rest are all relational in some way. Writing down those thirty things should be your first assignment.

When that is done, ask yourself if you have written down the twenty goals you need to achieve that life you described above. If not, that is your second assignment. The difference between the first, your dreams for your life, and the second, your goals for your life, is that the latter requires plans, is measurable, and is time-bound. There are called *SMART goals* (Specific, Measurable, Achievable, Realistically High, Time-bound). More on SMART goals can be found in appendix A, but here is an overview:

> SMART goals is a planning method for goal setting that has been used all over the world for decades. What makes it unique is that it goes beyond just writing down a goal and then trying to keep it going with your general efforts. SMART stands for:
>
> **S: Specific**
> The goal needs to be very specific, not general. Instead of *save more* use *save $1000 by the end of the year*.
>
> **M: Measurable**
> Use metrics, things you can measure, such as money or numbers.
>
> **A: Attainable**
> Make sure the goal is achievable for who you are and the resources you have.
>
> **R: Realistically High**
> Make it realistic, but a stretch goal, one that requires the best of who you are.
>
> **T: Time Bound**
> Put a specific date on the goal when you will achieve it.

In a real sense, there is nothing more important than those two assignments. Why? Because then, all of your life's choices, from daily, ordinary decisions to long-range decisions can be guided by those two lists.

In business terms, those two lists become the strategic plan for your life. All strategic plans are regularly reviewed for progress and change as the organization and the environment around it change.

Back to the quote. Those who do not know victory or defeat are most often timid out of fear, complacency, laziness, or cynicism.

The sad thing is that we all have some of those things within us. But the question is, do they dominate our heart and mind and inhibit our behavior? Can you identify those traits within you to some degree or in some areas of your life? To what degree do you let them inhibit your behavior and achievement of your goals and dreams?

You see, we can hide from those realities if we fear to look inwardly to make an honest and truthful assessment of ourselves.

If we fear to look inside to make that honest assessment, then how in the world can we know the weaknesses that will be traps and the strengths we can utilize to dare the mighty things that will help us achieve our potential as human beings?

Look to your potential, and then:

DARE MIGHTY THINGS!

Here is a revelation: if we do not take the time to look within, we walk into the battle of life totally disarmed in our unwillingness to assess who we are. We fall victim to our weaknesses and the momentary allurements that distract us from achieving our lofty goals.

Our culture today is diametrically opposed to that type of assessment. It is all out here on the exterior, on the surface, in the here and now, for fun, pleasure, and distraction.

That attitude keeps you solidly entrenched in the masses, easy to market to, whether by business, organizations, nonprofits, politicians, or whatever the movement of the day is. Easy prey in unthinking masses of followers is what they need, not independent thinkers who are in the culture but set themselves just a little apart. Notice I did not say *above*.

Pride and arrogance are still vices last time I checked. And humility is still a virtue.

They do not need or want people who are outliers. They do not want people who cannot be easily swayed or predictively marketed to after the focus groups tell them the right words to use. No, those people, the outliers, are a threat to the culture of mediocrity.

You already know that I am not talking about being rebellious against rightful authority or being anti-establishment or against tradition. Only the immature or fools disregard those in their rebellion.

Greatness arises from a true appreciation of the history and value of the things that actually bring a depth of understanding and wisdom, which of course is also quite contrary to the culture of today. As a matter of fact, I would counsel you to seek depth of understanding and wisdom in tradition, history, the establishments, and rightful moral authority.

This culture is so full of distractions that unless you find it within yourself to pull away to do that assessment, you will be handicapped in achieving your full human potential. Find wisdom where wisdom has borne fruit that is good, fruit that is positive and helpful to the human race.

But to know who you are interiorly is to be comfortable within your own skin. With all your current weakness and faults, you are working to correct them as well as draw upon your strengths. That is true humility, to know who you truly are in complete honesty and truth. That is strength.

When you do those things, assessing who you really are with complete humility, knowing intimately your strengths and weaknesses, when you set about writing down that word picture of your life and setting meaningful goals to achieve it, *then* you can look to your potential.

Finally, from that place, joy can be yours whether you know victory or defeat, pleasure or pain and suffering, success or failure. It is all just a part of the trip to achieving your potential.

Then you will be able to assess life for what it really is and

DARE MIGHTY THINGS!

You were created for it!

Go for it. You will never regret it, only if you do not try.

Dare to live fully!

DO 27 NOT 25 : HOT POINT 8

Those who dare to do mighty things in their lives may never be noticed by anyone but themselves and maybe by a few who are close to them. Mighty things might be overcoming incredible shortcomings or handicaps just to live a "normal" life. Only *you* know what is mighty and only you can define what is mighty for yourself. But the potential to dare what is mighty lies within you, no matter who you are, or what you are, or where you are. By the way, doing mighty things that the whole world notices starts there anyway!

1. Does the prospect of doing mighty things excite you and draw you in when it is put in the above perspective? Why?

2. What is it about daring mighty things causes you to pause, evokes fears or doubts? Why?

3. What are you going to do—specifically—about those things you identified in number two, above?

Do 27 Not 25 HOT Point Resolution. I will apply HOT Point 8, *Dare mighty things*, by writing down the mighty things I want to do with my life:

WEEK 9:

ONE OF THE MOST POWERFUL TOOLS YOU POSSESS

One of The Most Powerful Tools I Possess

One of the most powerful tools I possess is my ability to reflect. (The most powerful tool is my ability to love.)

It is my ability to reflect that gives me perspective of myself, my purpose, others and the world. Pursued with integrity, it reveals the truth, if I am open to it, about what is happening in my life and around me. It is my ability to reflect that gives me wisdom, insight, sound judgment and the eyes to see with the mind and heart what others miss.

When I take the time to reflect, I find my true purpose—to contribute to the wellbeing and happiness of others—and achieve my own happiness in the process.

If I take the time to reflect often—daily—alone, in silence if only for a few moments, then I will find I

am truly powerful—as I grow in the wisdom to live my true purpose.
It is in the silence that the chaos, noise, distractions, anxiety and confusion dies. Peace, calm and serenity appear in its place and the thread of truth that was being trampled is discovered.
Reflect and pursue the truth! The world needs it!
—Anonymous

"Hey professor, so what about love makes it the most powerful tool? The quote doesn't explain that."

Thanks for asking. You're sharp today.

Yes, the most powerful tool you possess is your ability to love. It's not emotional love, but the *decision* to love. I just wanted to clarify that. Love that makes sacrifices for the good of another. Love that is kind, considerate, does not put on airs, and is for the benefit of another. Be wary of emotional infatuation that masquerades as love for most people your age. It can be a trap that can hold you back from your development. Not what you want to hear maybe, right? I got it. Keep going.

True love seeks the good of the other, is willing to sacrifice for the other, helps the other be more, and does not use the other for selfish purpose. More on that another time, but you will need the capacity to love to drive the fire within to help all those who need what you have to give – the fullness of your potential.

ONE OF THE MOST POWERFUL TOOLS YOU POSSESS

The second most powerful tool you possess is your ability to reflect. This leads to the discussion of ethics in business—and in college and life for that matter. We all decry the lack of ethical conduct in business, politics, and relationships. But where do moral and ethical lapses come from?

They come from people who failed to adequately reflect on the consequences of their actions in light of a set of high moral standards.

By the way, what moral standards should you adopt for yourself? That is interesting, isn't it?

The moral standards of the culture?

Really?

In sociological terms that would be the lowest common denominator, wouldn't it? With *those* standards can you expect to be a success, to be apart from (not above, just a degree of objective separation) the culture, to dare mighty deeds, to *Do 27 not 25*?

Really?

Since when did you become delusional? Ha! Just kidding. Kinda, but you get my point.

For myself, I have chosen two things. First, transparency, twenty-four hours a day, 365 days a year. I do not do or say anything that I would not do or say to a customer, client, or my family and friends, twenty-four hours a day, 365 days a year. In other words, I remain transparent always and everywhere.

And the second, I have chosen the highest moral and ethical standards I am aware of. I am constantly looking to upgrade my standards for myself as I become more aware of my weaknesses and failures. I look for a higher standard to which I can strive.

Why those? It makes life so much easier and simpler when it comes to decisions about my actions and what I feel good about. Otherwise I have that accuser in the back of my head that I talked about earlier throwing stones at me and accusing me of my failures as a low life.

I am not perfect, not by a longshot, as I constantly fail those standards. However, I strive to live up to them, which satisfies my desire to live to my potential. I cannot rationalize a lower standard and desire it. That would be inconsistent and maybe schizophrenic?

OK, one more side trip. Unless you are a certified, bona fide, card-carrying, honest-to-God schizoid you are one person and *not* two.

"Say what, professor? What the ….?"

That means you cannot expect to have one set of moral standards for the job or at college and another set at home. You are one person, all the time. So tell me again what moral standards you have chosen for yourself and why?

To the quote: *reflection*. First, powerful tools and skills take a long time and hard work to develop. Some even take a good part of a lifetime. Look at those in your field or any other field like sports, medicine, or science and you will see the truth of that.

Second, the truth of any situation is usually not obvious, especially the more complex it is. It takes someone with keen insight honed over years to penetrate the fog and confusion, to get to the heart of the matter.

Our culture promotes the exact opposite. No truth, just opinion. All views are valid. There are no "objective moral norms," only moral relativism. But lying, murder, and stealing have always been wrong and always will be wrong. Those are called *objective moral norms*.

There are objective moral norms in this world, no matter how sophisticated and persuasive the arguments against them are. Culture hates objective moral norms because they imply standards of thought and behavior that are not susceptible to the whims of the pleasures of the moment or what is fashionable.

Stop!

Are you sure you want to go down this path of living to the fullness of your potential?

You are embarking on an Olympian journey if you keep going, my friend. It's much easier to throw in the towel and be mediocre with everyone else in the culture. Hey, there is the here and now to enjoy, after all.

"I am with you professor....."

You decided to read on? OK, but I warned you, my Olympian friend! Charge on.

Learn to:

REFLECT DAILY!

Consider this: truth is discoverable in relationships, in business, science, philosophy, religion, economics, engineering and every other field. For one who is trained in the art of reflection, truth is discovered more easily than for those who are constantly swayed by the culture because the popular culture wants nothing to do with the truth, by and large.

Society, popular culture, promotes plugged-in noise, entertainment, and distraction. But the ability to reflect, to discover, and to grow in wisdom requires the exact opposite: silence. And in that silence, thoughtful, careful reflection leads to uncommon insight and wisdom.

As the quote says, "It is in the silence, that the chaos, noise, distractions, anxiety and confusion dies. Peace, calm, and serenity appear and the thread of the truth that was being trampled is discovered." That journey and that capability is for you, if you chose it.

So, how do you do that? Take the time every day, at the start of every day, during the very first moments of your consciousness when you wake up, without any interruptions—no cell phone, music, TV, papers, people, your lover or anything else—to reflect before your mind and heart are filled with the legitimate concerns of the day. Start out with just five minutes and grow it over time. Nurture it carefully and it will grow.

ONE OF THE MOST POWERFUL TOOLS YOU POSSESS

That habit, done diligently every single day, will develop Olympic-sized reflection muscles that you can then easily use throughout the day when the chaos of normal daily life envelopes you. Finding a place for starting your day with silent reflection is a powerful helper. My place for doing that is an old easy chair in the living room. It gives me a place I can go to physically that makes it easier to go to the quiet place of reflection within me.

Don't mistake this for any new age spirituality, meditations, centering, or yoga, or other popular fads, which it definitely is not. This is about reflecting on who you are, what attitude you want to have for the day, what you will encounter in the day, and what is motivating you. It is about searching for the truth in all those situations.

Go to that physical place that is comfortable every morning, as soon as you wake up, close your eyes and reflect quietly within yourself. Let everything outside you evaporate into the background. Listen to your heart and breath. Find the place in you that is quiet and peaceful. Then be still.

After you find that interior space, rest there for a while. Stay there for a time.

Then afterward, it can help to find something to take with you to that place. I have some simple message that is uplifting and positive, yet challenging, that I get once a month. I read it every morning for the entire month. Take one of the quotes from this book, for instance.

Train yourself to be able to find the place of reflection within you by starting in that place every morning, at first for just five minutes. Then let the time you spend increase as you get more comfortable with it. Let it grow on you. As you know that place more and more, it will be easier to return there throughout the day.

Sooner or later, you will be able to stay in that reflective place throughout the day, no matter what is going on around you. And then you can pursue the truth in all situations from that place within you.

REFLECT DAILY!

Relentless searching for truth in all the situations is key; abandoning your biases and preferences, refusing the convenient solutions, is critical. Determine how you will react to what faces you and take responsibility for your thoughts and actions. Simply powerful!

Developing an ability to reflect by withdrawing to that place within you will yield great fruit as you see what most others miss. Then, whether you are in college, business, politics, education, nonprofits, parenting, or just being a friend or family member, your ability to reflect, developed over years and finely honed to a sharp skill will be a most powerful tool in your life skill set.

That tool will bring with it an uncommon insight to live as you have dreamed, to live to great and noble heights, even in the lowliest of occupations or circumstances, as our culture would paint them.

Do 27, not 25 when it comes to developing your ability to reflect.

REFLECT DAILY!

Develop your ability to reflect. You will never regret it, but I can assure you of this: if you do not develop it, you will bitterly regret it many times in your life.

"You got me on this one, professor. Already know that pain."

Then that's a good pain my friend. Remedy it by learning to reflect daily.

Reflect and find the truth!

DO 27 NOT 25 : HOT POINT 9

Reflecting is both an art form and a discipline that may sound simple, something people might talk about at lunch or at the bar. But few, very, very few, have a grasp of it or have the discipline to practice it consistently. You can literally see the evidence of it in their lives.

1. What is your attitude about the practice of taking the time for daily reflection? Why?

2. How will you set aside the time and space to do a daily reflection?

3. What benefits do you want from your daily reflection in the short term? How about in the long term? Be specific in your responses.

Do 27 Not 25 HOT Point Resolution. I will apply HOT Point 9, *Reflect daily,* by starting to reflect every day at the following time and place:

I will use the following source of inspirational reading after my time of reflection:

WEEK 10:

A WINNER'S BLUEPRINT FOR THE ACHIEVEMENT OF SUCCESS

A Winner's Blueprint for Achievement
Believe while others are doubting.
Plan while others are playing.
Study while others are sleeping.
Decide while others are delaying.
Prepare while others are daydreaming.
Begin while others are procrastinating.
Work while others are wishing.
Save while others are wasting.
Listen while others are talking.
Smile while others are pouting.
Commend while others are criticizing.
Persist while others are quitting.

—*William Arthur Ward*

"Hey, professor! This sounds like a lot of work. I came to college for fun. Man, if I do all this I am going to miss out on a lot, you know?"

Up to you, my friend. Whatever trips your trigger, I guess.

Kiss it off and go back to what you were doing. More fun that way. Be irresponsible. Why not? What's going to happen anyway? You'll get some kind of job when you graduate, probably...... maybe. That's what most people do, after all.

Work with me, will you? Humor me, OK? Play along and let's see where it goes. There might be something in this that it turns out you like.

The quote for this chapter is going to be used for something very different. We are going to turn this into a self-assessment.

Use the full page quote on the next page of the book and follow the instructions that I am about to give you to do the assessment. I have laid out the start of the assessment for you on the page and certainly you can use the page in the book to do the assessment.

You can also make a copy of the full page on a separate sheet of paper and then follow the instructions. I would recommend this method because you can hang it on the wall or keep it in a place in front of you.

When you make a copy, make several. Put the second copy away where you can dig it out at some point in the future, like a year from now, and do it again. See how you have improved or become a total degenerate. Ha!

A WINNER'S BLUEPRINT FOR THE ACHIEVEMENT OF SUCCESS

A Winner's Blueprint for Achievement Of Leadership Qualities

Virtuous Habits

Negative Habits

Believe while others are **doubting**.
+10 ———————— 0 ———————— -10
                    Average

Plan while others are **playing**.
+10 ———————— 0 ———————— -10
                    Average

Study while others are **sleeping**.
+10 ———————— 0 ———————— -10
                    Average

Decide while others are **delaying**.
+10 ———————— 0 ———————— -10
                    Average

Prepare while others are **daydreaming**.
+10 ———————— 0 ———————— -10
                    Average

Begin while others are **procrastinating**.
+10 ———————— 0 ———————— -10
                    Average

Work while others are **wishing**.
+10 ———————— 0 ———————— -10
                    Average

Save while others are **wasting**.
+10 ———————— 0 ———————— -10
                    Average

Listen while others are **talking**.
+10 ———————— 0 ———————— -10
                    Average

Smile while others are **pouting**.
+10 ———————— 0 ———————— -10
                    Average

Commend while others are **criticizing**.
+10 ———————— 0 ———————— -10
                    Average

Persist while others are **quitting**.
+10 ———————— 0 ———————— -10
                    Average

+120   x(me)=   O(others)=   -120

Adapted from the poem by William Arthur Ward

This quote presents a series of twelve stark contrasts.

Now, look at the double-underlined first word on each line. These are twelve constructive, positive and virtuous habits to develop for your whole life.

Now look at the last word on each line, with a single underline. They are twelve destructive, negative habits for your life and for your career.

As you look at the twelve and the contrast they represent, decide now to

BE KNOWN FOR VIRTUOUS HABITS

and not the others.

How do others describe you? Let's do the assessment. For each line of the poem, we are going to use a scale.

For each line, you can now score yourself from a positive ten to negative ten. For each line, put an X where you think you are: above average or below average, and how far above or below. Now put the number above the X that represents that positive or negative number on the scale. Once you have scored yourself on each line, go back to the top and think about all of your family and friends and how they would score you on that line and how far above or below average they would put you. Put an O (for *others*) on each line where others would say you are. Put the number above the O like you did for the X. Go to the bottom of the poem and on the left side you will see *+120* and a *-120* on the right. In the center left it says *X (me)=*. Add up your score. On the center right it says *O (others)=*. Add up your score.

If your score is 120, you walk on water! If your score adds up to a -120 you might consider joining a mercenary army in some far off land.

Looking at the difference between how you score yourself and how others score you might tell you that you need a reality check. Then, by looking at those scores, your score and those of others, and comparing them to the +120 tells you where development is needed and where your potential lies.

This assessment clearly shows you where you have to work.

Achievement is in not accepting mediocrity for yourself. Achievement is setting high standards and continuously working at attaining them. It requires self-confidence. You have to know yourself. It means taking a good hard look inside. Doing an honest self-assessment, setting progressively higher goals, and not accepting mediocrity for yourself is what achievement is all about.

Set high standards. And then go for those goals. Once you achieve them, reset them higher. Do it. Achieve according to the highest standards of personal conduct and leadership you can possibly conceive.

Can you look at each of the twelve constructive habits, identify them in yourself, and figure out what contributes to them? Can you think about how to reinforce each of them in yourself?

Can you, in the same way, take a look at the twelve negative habits and identify them in yourself in the degree to which they exist? We all have them to some degree. What within you causes them?

Ah, yes! This is harder work. The first was easy, this is harder. Confront the truth. Remember when we talked about cynicism, laziness, and indifference? Can you be truthful with yourself here?

Make a difference. Work your heart out to achieve these leadership qualities.

Whether you are an officially designated leader or not, you are still a leader in some respects, to someone, in fact to more people than you know. People look at you and observe the example you set.

I cannot tell you how many times people have come up to me and said how much I impacted them and their lives when I was not even conscious that I was doing anything out of the ordinary.

So it is with you. You are communicating to others, setting an example for others by who you are.

What kind of example are you?

Is it the absolute highest ideal that you know how to live? All the time?

Do 27, not 25.

BE KNOWN FOR VIRTUOUS HABITS!

Lead by example, not words. Let others see it in you.

It should go without saying, but great leaders are great followers first and foremost. Think about all it takes to be a great follower. Support the designated leader.

Do 27 Not 25 when it comes to being a follower.

Do your duty and then some. Not blindly, but wisely. If you have a conflict with your leader, deal with it quickly and discretely. All great leaders make mistakes, of course, so you need to be both tolerant and supportive.

The last thing any leader needs are insubordinate, unsupportive, lazy, or immoral followers. Great followers can make an average leader a great leader. I have seen that over and over again in my life.

If you want to learn something about being a great leader by being a great follower, read Jimmy Collins' book, "Creative Followership". As a matter of fact, jump straight to Chapter Two to get to the essence of the relationship between the leader and the creative follower.

Dare to be different.

The world is crying out for true leaders and true followers who are leaders in their own right.

BE KNOWN FOR VIRTUOUS HABITS!

If you are not going to be a true leader, then just tell me, who are you going to leave it to?

Think about that carefully. For my part, I would rather trust someone who is working on putting the principles of this book into practice than just about anyone else I can think of. The world needs your leadership.

Work on putting these principles to work in your life, then live it full out, to the best of your ability. When you fall short, as surely you will, get up the next day with resolve to do better.

Live a virtuous life and be known for your virtuous habits.

You will inspire others to be more than they are at present.

In your own small way, you will help lift up society to be more than it is at present.

Your virtuous habits will inspire others.

Be it!

DO 27 NOT 25 : HOT POINT 10

Well, if that is not a challenging list of virtuous leadership habits, I don't know what is! The interesting thing is, it is a set of very high standards, and few leaders have a conscious plan to work on their standards, which is why the world is wanting for good leaders. Of course the list is not comprehensive and there are better lists to be sure. But you cannot be a good leader without the qualities in that list.

1. What is your plan to develop yourself in each of the twelve traits?

2. Which of the twelve is the most challenging for you to work on and why?

3. Which of the twelve is a strength for you? How can you best use that trait?

Do 27 Not 25 HOT Point Resolution. I will apply HOT Point 10, *Be known for virtuous habits,* by assessing how I am doing on my plan in number one above to develop those habits on the following schedule:

WEEK 11:

DON'T QUIT

Don't Quit

When things go wrong, as they sometimes will,
When the road you're trudging seems all up hill,
When the funds are low and the debts are high,
And you want to smile, but you have to sigh,
When care is pressing you down a bit,
Rest, if you must—but don't you quit.

Life is erratic with its twists and turns,
As every one of us sometimes learns,
And many a failure turns about
When he might have won had he stuck it out;
Don't give up, though the pace seems slow—
You might succeed with another blow.

Often the goal is nearer than
It seems to a faint and faltering man,
Often the struggler has given up
When he learned too late, when the night slipped down,
How close he was to the golden crown.

> Success is failure turned inside out—
> The silver tint of clouds of doubt—
> And you never can tell how close you are,
> It may be near when it seems afar;
> So stick to the fight when you're hardest hit—
> It's when things seem worst that you must not quit.
>
> **—Anonymous**

"I got through the last one, professor. I actually got something out of it. Sometimes I think that with all the stuff I am involved in, this one might actually make some sense."

Glad you see that, too. You have experienced this in your life already, haven't you?

You remember when you were about to give up that one time but didn't. How did it turn out? Let's make that time a habit in your life now. Here it is:

PERSEVERE IN EVERYTHING!

We have talked about a lot of things this semester: writing down your dreams, what you want your life to be like, what you want out of your life, what you want your legacy to be.

Decide now what you want it to be. There is such an advantage to do that now because you can then map out the goals that will lead you to what you want.

Do you remember the ten to twenty goals you wrote? Do you remember SMART? If you take the time to do it, print it, and look at it on a consistent basis, it becomes a roadmap for your life. There are course corrections along the way naturally, as there is with any long-distance journey.

But *not* doing it will result in not achieving your dreams.

As the saying goes, "No map to anywhere will get you nowhere!"

We also talked about some new habits of thoughts this semester. This poem is about persistence and perseverance in the face of adverse circumstances outside yourself and in the face of internal obstacles. You will face both types of obstacles in achieving your dreams and adopting those new habits of thought.

PERSEVERE IN EVERYTHING!

The measure of your greatness as a human being in fulfilling your potential lies in your persistence, your perseverance in working at those habits of thought and action every day, in every circumstance, no matter what.

Doing it despite external obstacles, and even more so, despite internal obstacles, is what leads to greatness and success. Not the greatness and success that are measured by others, but the greatness and success that counts—that which brings meaning and fulfillment to you and those you love in your life.

Let me stop on that point. I suppose if you go back in my life you would discover people who might find it incredulous that I am writing such a book, as they knew me and my weaknesses, faults, and failures.

We all have those people in our lives, don't we?

But while I might be known to some more for my failures than for my successes and achievements, I have always fought to persevere in succeeding where it counted to me: in my physical, mental, emotional, spiritual, and family life.

Even if others judge me a failure according to their standards, it counts for nothing. They have no idea what I have had to overcome just to be what I am, poor as I might appear to be to them.

I am striving to live each one of the habits of thought I discuss in this book, to live to my fullest potential. That potential might be far below what someone else's is. Not everyone has the potential to be president or CEO. And that is OK. I do not need or even want the accolades of admirers. I need to be comfortable in my own skin and that's enough.

Success is exploring all the dimensions of my potential within myself and then striving every day to live to it. To me, that is exciting and energizing.

We talked in Chapter 10 about the internal assessment being the most difficult part of this book, but it is also where the biggest payoff is.

What is the best thing you can do for those you love, work with, or lead?

But of course: it is to achieve the fullness of your human potential.

The best gift you can give everyone outside yourself is to work very hard with everything you've got to fulfill your human potential.

That requires an uncommon degree of perseverance, courage, and an unrelenting focus on discovering the truth, whether it is within you or outside yourself.

Develop within you an uncommon mental toughness to stick with it, just over the edge of excellence, accepting the high personal price to be paid that goes with it.

PERSEVERE IN EVERYTHING!

You *will* become your habits of thought.

Those habits of thought will become your actions, right? It cannot be otherwise.

You *can* make the decision about what your habits of thought are.

No one else is going to make those decisions for you unless you abdicate those decisions to someone else. Like maybe the culture around you.

Really, you want to do that? You want to let the culture that exists for the unthinking crowds, for mediocrity, and for the lowest forms of behavior and ethics decide for you what your habits of thought will be?

Surely, it will decide your habits of thought if you do not decide otherwise and fight very hard, with a lot of discipline, to make your habits of thought what you intend them to be.

Re-read that again and let it sink in a minute.

Decide today, not tomorrow, what your habits of thought will be. Write them down. Look at them. Call them *affirmations* if you want.

Don't quit on yourself. Make those decisions every day, whether you succeeded or failed yesterday is irrelevant. Pick yourself up today and decide again.

PERSEVERE IN EVERYTHING!

Don't quit. Go for the gold that is your full potential as a human being.

Become the complete you.

Everyone will benefit—and you will too.

The world awaits you!

DO 27 NOT 25 : HOT POINT 11

Perseverance in everything. Sounds like a good thing to do, doesn't it? The problem is, we know the reality of trying to persevere in our lives is tough. So often, we just want to, and do, give up, just letting things happen. To persevere in everything takes an uncommon mental toughness that our culture strongly opposes. The whole of the culture is to go with the popular flow, not hanging tough on what is right, good, or hard. It is the challenge of the few who choose it.

1. Does the prospect of persevering in everything intimidate you or energize you? Why?

2. Can you identify the areas in your life where you are better at persevering? Why are you better at persevering in these areas?

3. Can you identify the areas in your life where you do not persevere, where you fail in living to your potential? Do you know why this is so?

Do 27 Not 25 HOT Point Resolution. I will apply HOT Point 11, *Persevere in everything,* by writing down the areas where I need to improve in my perseverance and a statement about what I will do for each:

WEEK 12:

CHILDREN (AND EMPLOYEES) LEARN WHAT THEY LIVE

CHILDREN LEARN WHAT THEY LIVE

If a child lives with criticism,
he learns to condemn.
If a child lives with hostility,
he learns to fight.
If a child lives with ridicule,
he learns to be shy.
If a child lives with shame,
he learns to feel guilty.
If a child lives with tolerance,
he learns to be patient.
If a child lives with encouragement,
he learns confidence.
If a child lives with praise,
he learns to appreciate.
If a child lives with fairness,
he learns justice.

> *If a child lives with security,*
> *he learns to have faith.*
> *If a child lives with approval,*
> *he learns to like himself.*
> *If a child lives with acceptance and friendship,*
> *he learns to find love in the world.*

—Dorothy L. Nolte

"Hey, professor Leis, this is getting a little personal, you know? I have some memories of growing up that… well, this brings up a lot of stuff for me."

Yea, I know. Believe me, I know. We will get to that issue. Stick with me.

This poem is fairly well known. Or at least it was a very, very long time ago, in a far-away galaxy….. or, uh, way back when I was middle-aged. (Love those Star Wars movies.)

My adaptation of it below rings just as true for employees, both in terms of how I was treated and how I saw others treated in my forty years of experience. I think it's just as true in terms of how I treated those who worked for me.

When you read the first part, what emotions did you feel?

I want you to stop right now and check your emotions.

Is there anger, frustration, joy, pleasantness, disappointment, resentment, love? Take a quick inventory and write a few reactions down.

Do it now.

Write down your first emotional reactions as you read those words.

Are you done? That's your basic set of dispositions, how you were formed as a child and how you matured.

That is a very important inventory to take. It tells you about the positive that you can build on. And it tells you about the negative things that you need to work at overcoming.

The worst place to be is to be blind or indifferent to those basic dispositions. In those places where you are blind to your basic dispositions and lacking in self-knowledge, you will be hampered by your ability to interact with people and the world around you. You will unconsciously be triggered by the past and how you were formed up to this point.

You have seen it many times in other people, when they act out of proportion to someone or something that triggered them. Their emotions overrule their thinking ability, their reason. Most likely, it has happened to you, right? That's old stuff triggering you that will get in your way and harm the relationships critical to your future. It points to where you need to work.

Take the inventory today and then go back and do it periodically in the future to measure the depth of your self-knowledge. After all, in your pursuit of the truth, it is paramount to discover the truth about yourself.

When I look at so many irrational, immoral, and even illegal actions by famous people, politicians, executives, friends, and most important, myself, I see that what was at the root of them was either a lack of self-knowledge or a self-knowledge that was not founded on truth.

In fact, for all their apparent success, many people have a profound lack of depth of self-knowledge grounded in truth. They live a perpetual façade, in fact. Those around them perpetuate the fantasy. You know it because you have seen it, particularly with famous people but also with popular people around you, even in your family.

I know. It has been me at times in my life, doing something that was irrational because I lacked the truth of who I was. It was humiliating in the end. The humiliation turned out to be a good thing as it led me to reflect on the situation.

If I have any claim to the virtue of humility at all, which in my case is questionable, it comes at the hand of humiliation in front of others. It's a small victory snatched from the jaws of defeat as it were.

Self-knowledge founded in truth puts a perspective on who I am, who I am in relation to others, and my rightful place in the world. Presumption, independence, and pride blind me to that.

CHILDREN (AND EMPLOYEES) LEARN WHAT THEY LIVE

So here is one for you: when you experience negative emotions or the humiliation of failure, don't shove it down and swallow it. Let it surface ever so carefully, experience it, turn it over like a rock and examine it from every side to see the dimensions of it. Be careful with it. It can be explosive until you disarm it.

You see, it is actually an emotional and perhaps psychological bomb as well. The way to disarm that experience of negative emotions and turn it into something useful, to learn from it, is to analyze it carefully. Look for the silver lining, the blessing that is contained within it for you. It is there if you work at it long enough and carefully enough. Relax in it, let it rise up in you, and then pass on through you like the wave that it is. Emotions come and go, so let this one pass as well. Never let your emotions control your actions.

Then you can take what you learn and turn it into pure gold! It becomes enriching as you embrace it and grow from it.

As you leave this part of the chapter, you know the truth of the old adage, "We are always creating a memory for someone." Memories were created for you, weren't they? Memories that were both good and bad, uplifting and demoralizing, healing and hurtful.

Be ever so careful about each memory you create for others. Seemingly little things can mean a lot more than you ever intended. There is no justification for creating negative memories most of the time.

Now let's take that into the next step, work.

Read the same poem and substitute the word *employee* in place of *child* as below:

EMPLOYEES LEARN WHAT THEY LIVE

If an employee lives with criticism,
he learns to condemn.
If an employee lives with hostility,
he learns to fight.
If an employee lives with ridicule,
he learns to be shy.
If an employee lives with shame,
he learns to feel guilty.
If an employee lives with tolerance,
he learns to be patient.
If an employee lives with encouragement,
he learns confidence.
If an employee lives with praise,
he learns to appreciate.
If an employee lives with fairness,
he learns justice.
If an employee lives with security,
he learns to have faith.
If an employee lives with approval,
he learns to like himself.
If an employee lives with acceptance and friendship,
he learns to find love in the world.

Adapted from poem by Dorothy L. Nolte

If you have had a job of any kind you have been on the receiving end of some, if not all of that, right? You know how it feels, both the positive and the negative.

Stop now to consider that after college, you will be in a position at some point to supervise others, perhaps almost immediately. Now look at those lines again. Can you be the kind of manager who is never guilty of the first four of those traits or other kinds of poor leadership traits? Can you be the kind of manager who is always and consistently practicing the last seven traits and the other characteristics of good leaders?

The HOT Point, *Do 27 not 25!* says you take some serious time out of your life to look at them and form strategies around how you look at and value yourself and how you will react and interact with the world around you.

In this way, you become a leader because you know yourself well and conduct yourself well. You lead silently first and foremost. When you do open your mouth, you are conscious of the principles these poems teach.

To paraphrase Maya Angelou: people may not remember what you said, but they will always remember how you made them feel.

And how you make them feel has a huge bearing on your leadership effectiveness and the willingness of people to follow you.

Take those last two sentences and put them somewhere you can see them again.

Moving from the first to the second version of the poem is now the challenge of "becoming." What was in the past versus what you need to become. Once you have evaluated who and where you are, then it is the time for becoming. Now is the time to plan on who and what you need to become. And then you have to decide what it is going to take to get there.

From the beginning of this book we have talked about becoming. The need is to work on *who* and *what* you need to be for what is ahead of you.

There is a certain *leaning forward* disposition required here that brings a degree of uncommon maturity and perspective, which most of your peers do not have in our culture.

LEAN FORWARD INTO BECOMING!

Think of a runner or downhill skier. There is a "leaning forward" as they press the race. So it is with you. Your disposition should be one of leaning forward, leaning into the race to become who and what you need to become.

You are who you are at the moment and there is nothing you can do about the past, either good or bad. But you can use those experiences and learn from them.

You can become who and what you need to become to live to your potential and to live for what is in front of you. What a marvelous gift it is for you and for everyone around you!

LEAN FORWARD INTO BECOMING!

Now you can look at yourself in truth (that's critical) with a certain degree of detachment as you grow into becoming what you need to be.

Look forward to those hopes, dreams, goals, and everything that has to change so that you can be what you are capable of being.

That's exciting and invigorating.

And a gift!

DO 27 NOT 25 : HOT POINT 12

You took an inventory of your basic disposition and wrote down your reactions to the lines in the poem. What if it was not a poem but a person saying those things to you? As you interact with the world around you, that will happen. It is good to take note of your reactions and consider what is prompting them, as it gives you clues about your disposition. Knowing those reactions and their source within you gives you the knowledge to manage and control them, not the other way around. Now you can manage others effectively.

1. Do you ever find yourself reacting to something and then later wondering why you reacted that way? Describe what happened.

2. You now have a small set of leadership behaviors as a model. Do you have other traits or behaviors to add to the list the poem presents? Take this opportunity to list them.

3. How might you go about leaning forward into becoming in some pragmatic ways?

Do 27 Not 25 HOT Point Resolution. I will apply HOT Point 12, *Lean forward into becoming,* **by adopting the following resolutions in my life:**

WEEK 13:

CONSULT NOT YOUR FEARS

Your Potential

Consult not your fears,
  but your hopes and dreams.

Think not about your frustrations,
  but about your unfulfilled potential.

Concern yourself not with what you have tried and failed in,
  but with what it is still possible for you to do.

—*Angelo Giuseppe Roncalli*

"Easy for you to say, professor. But I get you. I have read this far, right?"

Yes, congratulations on hanging in there with me. At this point in your journey, you probably already know what I am going to say about this, right? Read on!

As you move from moment to moment, day to day, and year to year, you will encounter your fears, because that is a very normal part of being human. But just because you encounter fear does not mean that you need to do anything more than just acknowledge it.

You do not need to let fear control your thoughts or actions.

Really.

To paraphrase Ambrose Redmoon, "Courage is not having no fear. It is going on despite the fear."

Speak to large groups, climb high mountains figuratively and literally, dare mighty deeds, explore the dimensions of humility, display kindness to the unloved, go for that job or promotion, and start that company!

It is your noble hopes and dreams that should guide your thoughts and actions.

The pop culture kills the pure hopes and dreams of children and substitutes the empty promises of pleasure and consumption of "stuff" that it needs to perpetuate itself. Like addicts on drugs, the vast majority in our culture want more and more, to the point of becoming unethical and even violent if they do not get what they want.

Everything in the current culture that serves to get your attention in the here and now, all those things easily 'find' you and distract you. They have little positive and maybe even negative value to you living your unfulfilled potential.

The things that are of high value to your long term achievement and success, to living your unfulfilled potential, you have to search out, you have to prioritize over those things that vie for your attention in the here and now. And you have to do it day by day, minute by minute. Most succumb to the here and now.

Read those last two paragraphs again, carefully. What is pulling at you to get your attention in the here and now is likely not contributing to your long term achievement of your potential. Think carefully about what you pay attention to during your day. Eliminate what is not beneficial to where you are headed, as good or entertaining or distracting as they may be.

But you can choose to be different. You can choose to have as your focus and goal to

LIVE YOUR UNFULFILLED POTENTIAL!

You have not even scratched the surface of realizing your unfulfilled potential. How could you? You have not fathomed your own depths yet. This book is only opening the door to that exploration, and what an exciting journey it is! For the rest of your life it can invigorate you every day. Really.

I am several times your age and I live excited and invigorated every day, no matter how tired I am or what else is going on in my life. You can too. Really. No BS!

But you have to want it and *Do 27 Not 25* to get it. It does not happen naturally, you have to work at it to make it happen. In fact, you will have to fight to train the very nature of your humanity.

LIVE YOUR UNFULFILLED POTENTIAL

and it will energize your life and those around you.

Forget what you have failed at. Forget what others have told you that you have failed at or will fail at.

Those past failures may not have been failures if you see them in a new light, as having been part of your character formation. You learned and grew from them. I have said since I was a young man, "There are no failures, just learning experiences" (paraphrased from Tom Krause I think).

Stop focusing on the past and the condemnation or negativity that comes from it. I carry around a coin in my pocket that was given to me by Bill Bartmann, the famous entrepreneur, lawyer, and billionaire. On one side it says, "Never be intimidated by failure." And on the other side, "Never be awed by success." They are two sides of the same coin: you. He should know, he's had more of both failure and success than ten people put together.

I strongly suggest you check out Appendix D on dealing with failure. Guess what? You are going to fail, maybe even in a spectacular way like he did and I have. You will need to know how to deal with that as much or more than dealing with success! I also think his book,

"Bouncing Back" should be required reading for all college students (profits go to charity, I think).

And as for those future failures, those learning experiences? Sure you will have them. And for those who are pursuing their unfulfilled potential with gusto and vigor, you will have lots of failures to teach you. No worry. Press on anyway.

So press on my friend!

LIVE YOUR UNFULFILLED POTENTIAL!

Remember that the achievement of that lofty goal requires an extraordinary degree of self-knowledge and perseverance we have talked about.

Resolve now to know your strengths and weaknesses, what triggers you, and how you were formed psychologically and emotionally. Know how committed you are to discovering the truth of every situation no matter the consequences, what motivates you, what your talents and skills are, and what you need to develop.

Above all, you must cultivate an uncommon degree of humility, which is simply a very truthful knowledge of self.

Leave your fears behind and strike out in new areas that you had once fancifully considered but decided against because of fear, doubts about your ability, or the negativity of others. How else will you explore the dimensions of your unfulfilled potential unless you do those things?

Let me give you a very common example from my classrooms: many times when I ask a student early in the semester to stand up and read something, or provide a detailed answer to a problem, I get a reluctant response.

That reluctance indicates to me and to them an area where they need development. So I point that out to them and encourage them to step forward into the challenge of doing it voluntarily, and frequently enough that they become comfortable with it. It never fails. They see the challenge and rise to it for the rest of the semester. I use that experience as a teaching tool regarding identifying their need for self-development and overcoming fear.

The point is, if that is you in any type of new, expanding type experience, then you know that is something you need to develop and not, repeat, not shrink back from. Get it? That's when you know you have a developmental opportunity staring you in the face. Go for it! Leave your fears behind to grasp the opportunity to live to your potential!

And if you try something and fail, look carefully. Make sure you do not stop because of fear. You did not learn to ride a bicycle or drive a car the first time out.

Failure does not mean you should not go on with your attempts. It just means just the opposite: you either did not try the right way or at the right time. Jump back on the bicycle!

Push into new areas in every dimension of your life to explore your unfulfilled potential. In some ways you will succeed. And when you fail, that is just part of the journey, right? I have often discovered that there was a proverbial silver lining in every one of my failures that resulted in something really good. Look for it.

Look with unbridled optimism to your future and what is still possible for you to do, no matter what has happened in the past.

LIVE YOUR UNFULFILLED POTENTIAL!

Press on to the future.

It is bright beyond your imagining if you want it to be.

And your example will help so many who desperately need to see it in you because they cannot see it in themselves.

Press on!

DO 27 NOT 25 : HOT POINT 13

To live your life in such a way as to realize your unfulfilled potential sounds like a wonderful thing, and surely it is. But that goal is elusive for the vast majority of the population. Rather, they settle for something far less, trading that lofty goal for just getting by. Why is that?

1. Do you think that you have what it takes within you to live your unfulfilled potential?

2. What is it about living your unfilled potential that causes you to pause, that evokes fear or doubts?

3. What are you going to do about those things you identified in number two, above?

Do 27 Not 25 HOT Point Resolution. I will apply HOT Point 13, *Live your unfulfilled potential,* **by doing the following things to explore the dimensions of my unfulfilled potential:**

WEEK 14:

THAT SPARK OF INSPIRATION WITHIN YOU?

The Spark of Inspiration

That spark of inspiration

within you?

Fan it into a flame!

Live an inspired life!

And then

Do 27 not 25!

—David A. Leis

"So I finally get a quote from you, professor? Wondered when I would see one from you."

Yep. I could not hide this one. It's mine, which means I am held to it and measured by it. You can challenge me to it when we meet. The pressure is on me, huh? But let's go on.

You have felt the spark of inspiration before, right? During a talk some place, watching an inspiring movie or TV show, reading an article some place, or seeing someone achieve something difficult. Or maybe as you read this book, for instance.

What happened to that spark of inspiration within you?

Stop right here for a moment. Put the book down and think about it.

What did you do with that spark you felt? Did you make a decision, or did it just happen and then die in the rush of everyday life?

Here is an alternative. Make a firm decision and act on it. Now. Develop a plan.

That spark of inspiration you feel right now? Turn it into a flame.

Don't let it go by. Don't spill the fine wine. Don't let the wisp of wind carry the beautiful flower out of your reach. Don't drop the precious jewel in the ocean.

Grasp it gently but surely. Examine the spark you felt within you like you would a beautiful flower or jewel. And then take possession of it and protect it.

Don't let the thieves of our culture rob it from you with their mediocrity and empty promises.

Nurture the spark into a flame, burning brightly within you.

Decide to

LIVE AN INSPIRED LIFE

with the spark of inspiration turned into a flame. People will see it in your eyes and in your actions. Your mind and heart will be filled with an electrum, an energy beyond description as you engage all of life.

You will cause others to wonder and maybe even ask. And maybe they will catch onto it from you.

Then, *do 27 not 25!*

Do it your whole life,

LIVE AN INSPIRED LIFE

each and every day, no matter what the trials and tribulations are, because you decided how you would live the day.

You woke up and went straight into a time of reflection.

You chose to decide what your attitude was going to be today.

You chose to *do 27 and not 25* in every aspect of your life.

You chose to live this day transparently, ethically, and joyfully, no matter how you felt internally, for the good of others around you, whether emotionally you feel 'happy' or not, rested or not.

You made sure to take care of your own physical, emotional, mental, and spiritual needs properly so that you could continue living that inspired life and help others do it. Don't go dysfunctional on me now, OK? The world awaits you, but you need to be whole and healthy in all aspects of your life, right?

You live in the culture, as we all do. But you have chosen to be just a little apart from (detached from) it to protect who you are and who you dream you want to become.

Live to your potential—it's the greatest gift you can give the rest of us.

Fan the spark of inspiration within you into a flame!

DO 27 NOT 25! LIVE AN INSPIRED LIFE!

Today.
    Every day.
    For the rest of your life!
    The whole world needs you to rise to the challenge!

DO 27 NOT 25 : HOT POINT 14

Living an inspired life is not normally the result of a one-time event, a single inspiration, but rather the result of living expectantly, knowing that the spark of inspiration will come and then acting on it. Acting on it over and over again. With some successes and some failure. Sometimes there may be more failures in acting on the inspirations than successes. Not to worry. It is just a matter of fine tuning your ability to act on the inspiration. But the outcome of the inspiration should not impact your ability to live an inspired life because inspiration is an attitude, a way of living, a disposition. And that is something you can choose every day!

1. What does it mean for you to live an inspired life? In other words, what does it look like and feel like?

2. Do you know that place within your heart and mind where the spark can be fanned

into a flame? Describe it in as much detail as you can.

3. Can you recall the last few times you felt a spark of inspiration? What happened to each of them?

Do 27 Not 25 HOT Point Resolution. I will apply HOT Point 14, *Live an inspired life*, by writing down two things that have inspired me in the last few weeks. And then for each inspiration, I will write what I want to do:

THAT SPARK OF INSPIRATION WITHIN YOU?

The Succeed Wildly™
Habits of Thought (HOT) Points™

My Destiny is HOT!

Do 27 Not 25!™

Guard the First Minutes of Consciousness

Focus on the Needs of Others

Choose Belief in Yourself

Adopt an Attitude of Continuous Improvement

Make No Excuses

Bear Good Fruit

Dare Mighty Things

Reflect Daily

Be Known for Virtuous Habits

Persevere in Everything

Lean Forward into Becoming

Live Your Unfulfilled Potential!

Live an Inspired Life!

TAKE *DO 27 NOT 25!* TO THE NEXT LEVEL

The following appendices on dreams and goal-setting are the first steps to taking what you have learned here to the next level. You have the basic attitudes, habits of thought, and behaviors from working the program to this point. The appendix on failure is critical too, as you will encounter failure, maybe more than success.

Now let's put some muscle into them by committing to paper the dreams, goals, and action plans to get you where you want to go in some pragmatic ways.

By the way, there is a method to my madness here, wouldn't you guess? First, I have these appendices here (as opposed to within the chapters) because these should be worked on starting with the first week and continued throughout your time working on the program. So the next two chapters are appendices because they float over all the chapters.

Secondly, the secret is, if you learn to master dreams, goal-setting and action plans for yourself, those skills are directly transferable to your work environment. Amazingly, they are skills that few possess. By working on them in your personal life, where they have immediate meaning and benefit, you will have the maximum motivation to master these skills. Then it will be second nature to you in the work environment. You will have a leg up on your competition. And of course, the fact that you have mastered these skills in college means that you will have lots of accomplishments during your time in college to add to your resume when you are looking for that job.

A few other notes before you jump into dreams, goal-setting, and action plans:

The *Do 27 Not 25!* philosophy of living is supported by a growing community of organizations and services. Visit our website often to get the latest updates.

Succeed Wildly Planner and Notebook: Available separately, this companion planner and notebook reinforces the success principles and provides space for notes, dreams, goals, HOT Point answers, and HOT Resolutions. It also contains a lot of forms for goal-planning and action plans, as well as other information on prioritizing goals.

Free Offers: We like free! Check our website for the latest free offers and resources as we are always adding something: www.succeedwildlyincollege.com

Cool Stuff: Check the web site for cool stuff we will be offering in the future, like wrist bands, T-shirts, and pens.

APPENDIX A:
THE DREAMS FOR YOUR LIFE

Before you can effectively set goals for your life, it is important for you to know what you want from your life, both in the short term and the long term. If you ordered the *Personal Planner and Notebook*, it has space for you to fill all that in, as it was outlined in the Warm Up Exercise. Forms are also available on the website: www.succeedwildlyincollege.com

But let's at least get you thinking:

1. The twenty dreams for your life. Write a sentence or two for each:

2. The ten dreams you have for your time at college:

3. What ten things do you want most from your college education? What benefits?

Spend some quality time with these dreams. Create pictures in your mind of what the experience of living those dreams would be like. Feel the feelings. Even make some artwork pages and post them in your room. Now, ask yourself these questions and then revise your list.

   A. Are the dreams you have for your life worth the effort you need to put into them or are they just fanciful dreams?

   B. What effort are you willing to put into working toward these dreams?

   C. Is it important that you have someone else involved in helping you realize these dreams?

   D. Who would want to help you with each dream and why?

It's a lot to think about for each dream, but a very small amount of work now will tell you which dreams are worth your attention and which are simply fanciful flights of imagination and not worth spending time on.

APPENDIX B:
SMART GOALS AND GOAL-SETTING

Once you have those dreams written out, it is time to set some goals to move you toward those dreams. You do not, as a result of the goal-planning, have to accomplish the dream, but the goal should make a material contribution to helping you achieve the dream. Say for instance your dream while you are at college is to participate in an ironman competition by the time you are a junior. Well, you might have to set a dozen goals just to help you get there (running goals, swimming goals, workout goals). Get it?

So let's talk about how to set goals. SMART is a planning method for goal-setting that has been used all over the world for decades. What makes it unique is that it goes beyond just writing down a goal and then trying to keep it going with your general efforts.

SMART stands for:
S: Specific
The goal needs to be very specific, not general. Instead of *save more* use *save $1000 by the end of the year.* The more specific it is, the better.

M: Measurable
Use metrics, things you can measure, (money, numbers, and so on). If someone else can measure it, then it's measurable! Weigh 140 pounds, save $3000, do one hundred sit-ups, run five miles, achieve a 3.7 GPA.

A: Attainable and Achievable
Make sure the goal is achievable for who you are and the resources you have. Make it doable.

R: Realistically high
Make it a stretch goal. A goal that requires the very best of you. No easy goals here!

T: Time-bound
Create a date for when you will achieve the goal.

APPENDIX B: SMART GOALS AND GOAL-SETTING

So a poor goal might be stated as, "Get better grades."

A good SMART goal might read, "Put at least two hours a night into MT 101 study and office hours visits to get my grade to a B by the midterm on October, 20, 20__."

Or "Work out in the gym every weekday morning from 6:00 to 6:30 a.m. the first and second semester until finals in May 2015."

Now for each of those dreams, you need to set at least one SMART goal. Let's set those SMART goals so they can be accomplished over a short time horizon, like the next six months. In a rare instance, you might make them a year out, but you need goals that you can accomplish in the short term. Often times ninety-day goals are best.

Life Balance and Goals

But before you start setting goals, let's do an evaluation. Rate yourself in the following areas in terms of how you are doing versus how you want to be. Rate yourself from zero (not even started) to ten (I am achieving all I could hope to in this area at this point in my life).

1. Financial
2. Academic and Intellectual
3. Health and Fitness
4. Relationships and Social
5. Family
6. Spiritual and Ethical
7. Contributions to Others

For those areas that you rated less than ten, you should be setting goals. There is a whole science to setting goals and achieving them that goes beyond what can be dealt with in this book. But you can check out the website, www.succeedwildlyincollege.com, for more information.

Your success in achieving your dreams and goals, which will change with time, is dependent on you mastering the techniques of goal-setting and achievement.

Master Goal-setting!
OK, now you have a list of goals. Let's talk about how to pragmatically go after each of them. First, for each goal, I want you to list one or two benefits of achieving the goal or a feeling you will get when you achieve the goal.

Like that $3000 you want to save? The benefit is a down-payment on a used car. Freedom! I feel great cruising the streets. See, if you write your goal and then the benefits, you get your emotions hooked into it. Now motivation will come naturally when trying to achieve the goal.

But there is one more thing. Yeah, I know. "Hey professor, this is feeling like homework, you know?" Stick with me, OK? Just a moment longer. This goal-setting stuff is really, really important now in college, but more so in your career.

The last part before we start planning out the goal is to write down the consequences you will experience if the goal is *not* achieved. What pain, suffering, or loss will you experience? This is important too, as you can imagine. Sometimes pain, suffering, and loss are negative motivations sufficient to keep us moving in the right direction.

So here is what you should have created and evaluated:
1. Your dreams.
2. Your goals in each of the seven life-balance and goal areas to achieve those dreams.
    a. benefits of achieving the goal
    b. consequences of not achieving the goal.

Next up is the key to realizing your dreams and goals. Developing and implementing action plans for each is a skill that every successful person has mastered. Therefore, number three will be *action plans for each goal.*

APPENDIX C: ACTION PLANS

Now for item three, action plans, there is a very simple technique. Write the specific action step that is needed, its priority (A, B or C), by when it needs to be done, and its status. You can create a sheet for each goal that has all of this information. Forms are available in the *Personal Planner and Notebook* and on the website www.succeedwildlyincollege.com

SMART Goal:					
Benefits:					
Consequences:					
Step #	Action Step	Priority	Person Responsible	Due Date	Status

Now, go *Do 27 Not 25!* when it comes to the dreams and goals exercises. I can guarantee you that no map to anywhere will get you nowhere.

You take the time to plan vacations, right? Then take some time to plan out and map out your life! It is certainly more important than a vacation.

I can also guarantee you that if you put in the time and effort to do all this work and review your goals every week, you will make more progress than you ever thought possible.

Remember that we are talking about making an adjustment of your trajectory, the current course that you are on, not a wholesale complete revolution. I have some students who have done exactly that with spectacular results, however!

Like a flight from New York to Moscow—make a small adjustment at the beginning and you end up in Sydney, Australia enjoying the beaches, balloon rides, and the outback instead of snow and ice.

Make sure you resolve to review your goals every week and determine what actions you can take on a daily basis to advance one or more of the goals. I actually plan out each of my weeks on a spreadsheet. I will share that with you on the website as well. For each day, I list the action steps I want to accomplish for the day in terms of the goals I am working on. Not too many, just what I think I can reasonably get done, *plus two*! LOL! Got it?

APPENDIX C: ACTION PLANS

Sunday	Monday	Tuesday	Wednesday	Thursday	Friday	Saturday
1.						
2.						
3.						
4.						

These are the basic tools you need to begin realizing your dreams by accomplishing your goals. A note of caution here from my military experience: no plan for a battle gets executed as envisioned, the enemy is unpredictable. So it is with our lives. No set of dreams, goals, and plans once committed to paper gets executed as planned. Life is unpredictable. Roll with it. Make adjustments. The weather will affect the flight path of the plane on its trip from New York and adjustments have to be made.

APPENDIX D: DEALING WITH FAILURE

As my friend Bill Bartmann, CEO of CFSII says, failure is something most people do not teach but something all of us have to deal with.

You see, Bill has had more failures and more successes than a dozen or maybe a hundred men, certainly more than anyone else I have ever met. Last time I checked, he was well on his way to becoming a billionaire. Again. And he has been a millionaire a few times. And completely broke in between those times.

If you want an interesting read, visit his website www.billbartmann.com and you will get a sense of who he is. The guy who was attacked by the Attorney General of the United States was praised by Mother Teresa! All wrapped up in one amazing guy.

But for now, it is his failures, my failures, and your failures I want to concentrate on. We are all going to have failure in our lives and some of us will have a lot. I addressed this topic in the text a little, but I think it bears repeating and expanding on.

Bill gave me a coin that I have carried in my pocket every day for years. On one side it says, "Never be intimidated by failure," and on the other side, it says,

"Never be awed by success." I put my hand on it many times a day and each time it triggers that message, now subconsciously.

In other words, never let yourself be intimidated or stopped by your failures. I have always called them *challenges* and learning experiences. You might have to dig down deep to find the courage or strength to keep going if the failure is a significant one, but that just builds character, mental muscle, and wisdom. The wrong answer is fear and paralysis.

Yes, you will have fear, but that is just an emotion and not your willpower. Find the courage to drive on despite the failure. I have had a lot of spectacular failures, believe me.

If the failure brings humiliation, all the better. For most of us, unlike Mother Teresa of Calcutta, humility does not come easily or naturally. It comes by way of the experience of humiliation. So let it have its positive effects that way as well.

On the other hand, don't get full of yourself and awed by your successes. In most cases, those successes had others contributing to your efforts and there was probably some luck or good timing involved. Besides, pride is always a vice.

It is great to be proud of your successes in life and you need to go after the next one. But when you take pride in yourself—in what you have, own, accomplish, look like—or when your pride causes you to look at any other person as less, then it is toxic pride. It will eventually poison you and your relationships. You are simply no better or worse than the next person.

Bottom line: take your failures in stride. They are just a part of life, one of the two sides of life, like one of the two sides of Bill Bartmann's coin.

Go buy his book, "Bouncing Back." It is a quick easy read, full of amazing lessons you will not forget. I highly recommend it, and if I recall, all the profits go to charity anyway.

Never be intimidated or paralyzed by your failures. They can teach you much.

Stay focused on living to your potential as the greatest gift you can give to others.

ABOUT THE AUTHOR

David Leis is an award-winning consultant, author, speaker, trainer, executive coach, and college instructor. For over thirty years he has spoken and trained thousands of people in a wide variety of settings, from colleges to the Fortune 500 businesses to small companies to nonprofits around the globe.

His company, Avantt Consulting, founded in 1991, has won a number of awards, including New York State Small Business Development *Growth Company of the Year*.

David has extensive experience in the areas of strategic planning, marketing, new product development, sales, project management, government contracting, software development, IT systems, and education and training. He has authored a number of publications, including a new product development manual, a performance counseling and review manual, and a manual used to develop proposals for government contracts. In addition, he has authored several human resources courses and training programs in the areas of teamwork, personal communications, marriage and family life, and an eighty-hour train-the-trainer course in diversity.

As both a full-time and adjunct professor, he has taught thousands of students in a half dozen different colleges from New York City to upstate New York.

His passion is helping people and organizations grow beyond their wildest expectations. As a highly rated full-time and adjunct professor, he helped thousands of students achieve far more in college than they ever thought possible, helping them land jobs they never considered feasible. David has done executive coaching for college students, small business owners, middle market companies, and executives of Fortune and Global 500 companies (including divisions of Corning, Japanese & US executives of Toshiba, GE, RCA and others). He has appeared on TV, in newspapers, and in trade journals.

David is a graduate of West Point and the University of Southern California, and has done coursework on an MBA at Syracuse University and on a PhD at Rutgers. Previously, David was airborne, ranger, and a company commander in the US Army and a Top 100 executive of Harris (a Fortune 500 and on the fast-track lists at RCA and GE).

David's adventurous life has included climbing mountains in Colorado, running from the bulls in Pamplona, Spain (and dodging them in the bull ring), parachute jumping from airplanes, rappelling from

ABOUT THE AUTHOR

cliffs and helicopters, hunting and fishing across the United States, riding bulls in rodeos, a number of survival courses, motorcycle riding, flying an airplane for a few terrifying minutes, glider and hot air balloon excursions, fresh water and ocean water skiing, and traveling in thirty-four countries, including walking the Great Wall of China.

As a serial entrepreneur, David started his first company at age eight, when he took a loan from his hometown bank to start a lawn-mowing company. It allowed him to have his first motorcycle and car when he turned fourteen, then the legal driving age in Kansas. He has helped launch over a dozen companies and help to merge several successfully.

David has served on the boards of nonprofit organizations and companies and currently serves on a board with former governor (and DHS secretary) Tom Ridge, General Wesley Clark, former NATO commander and US presidential candidate, and Mike Bowman, recipient of president Obama's *Challenge Award*. David also served on former congressman and Corning CEO Amory Houghton's Service Academy Selection Committee for selecting candidates for West Point and the Naval, Air Force, and Merchant Marine Academies.

David lives near Princeton, New Jersey with his two sons and close to his daughter's family in Connecticut. He has donated his services to civic and religious organizations that serve the disabled and the poor.

www.ingramcontent.com/pod-product-compliance
Lightning Source LLC
LaVergne TN
LVHW051830080426
835512LV00018B/2801